TEACHER GUIDE

Includes Stude[nt]
Worksheets

4th–6th Grade

History

Answer Key

Timeline of the Revolution

MASTER BOOKS
— CURRICULUM —

Authors: Rick & Marilyn Boyer

Master Books Creative Team:

Editor: Craig Froman

Design: Terry White

Cover Design: Diana Bogardus

Copy Editors:
Judy Lewis
Willow Meek

Curriculum Review:
Kristen Pratt
Laura Welch
Diana Bogardus

First printing: November 2015
Fourth printing: August 2020

Master Books®, P.O. Box 726, Green Forest, AR 72638
Master Books® is a division of the New Leaf Publishing Group, Inc.

ISBN: 978-0-89051-911-0
ISBN: 978-1-61458-486-5 (digital)

Unless otherwise noted, Scripture quotations are from the New King James Version of the Bible.

Printed in the United States of America

Please visit our website for other great titles:
www.masterbooks.com

For information regarding author interviews,
please contact the publicity department at (870) 438-5288.

Rick and Marilyn Boyer were among the pioneers of the modern home education movement in the early 1980s. Together they founded The Learning Parent ministry, have written over a dozen books, and travel around the country and abroad, speaking at home-school and Christian parenting conferences to encourage, inspire, and challenge the parents straining the next generation of Americans. Their books have circulated around the globe and have been translated into several foreign languages.

Affordable
Flexible
Faith Building

MASTERBOOKS
—CURRICULUM—

Table of Contents

Author Bio:
Rick and Marilyn Boyer have a decades-long love affair with American history. Marilyn is the author of the highly acclaimed book, *For You They Signed*, an in-depth study of the signers of the Declaration of Independence. Rick is known to thousands of children across America as "Uncle Rick the Storyteller" through his many historical audio books and storytelling CDs. The Boyers are nationally known homeschool speakers and authors. They are also among the pioneers of the modern home education movement. Beginning in 1980, they have homeschooled all of their 14 children from kindergarten through high school. They have also written around a dozen parenting books and are in demand as speakers for homeschooling and parenting conferences. Their speaking ministry has taken them to nearly every state in the union and several foreign countries.

Using This Teacher Guide

Features: The suggested weekly schedule enclosed has easy-to-manage lessons that guide the reading, worksheets, and all assessments. The pages of this guide are perforated and three-hole punched so materials are easy to tear out, hand out, grade, and store. Teachers are encouraged to adjust the schedule and materials needed in order to best work within their unique educational program.

Lesson Scheduling: Students are instructed to read the pages in their book and then complete the corresponding section provided by the teacher. Assessments that may include worksheets, activities, quizzes, and tests are given at regular intervals with space to record each grade. Space is provided on the weekly schedule for assignment dates, and flexibility in scheduling is encouraged. Teachers may adapt the scheduled days per each unique student situation. As the student completes each assignment, this can be marked with an "X" in the box.

🕐	Approximately 30 to 45 minutes per lesson, five days a week
🔑	Includes answer keys for worksheets and quizzes
✏️	Worksheets for each section
📄	Quizzes are included to help reinforce learning and provide assessment opportunities
🔄	Designed for grades 4 to 6 in a one-year course

Course Objectives: Students completing this course will

- Investigate the causes of the War for Independence
- Become familiar with the first battles of the revolution
- Identify leaders of the war and see God's hand at work in the formation of the American people
- Learn how the early American army went from weakness to strength as the battles raged around them
- Study the turning points of the revolution and the people who were vital to victory

Course Description

This course prepares students to experience the struggles and triumphs of the many who committed their lives, fortunes, and sacred honor to build the foundations of freedom and faith we have inherited. Students will explore the causes of the Revolutionary War, follow along as leaders are chosen and battles are fought, and learn how the United States of America was established as a new nation. This is a distinctive study of American history from the Revolutionary War to the ratification of the Constitution. Students discover in-depth character comments, explanations of providential occurrences, Founders' quotes, and poetry from the time period.

This Teacher Guide is designed for use with *America's Struggle to Become a Nation*, 4th to 6th grade history text. We suggest reading selections on Monday, Tuesday, and Wednesday. Projects are supplied to be completed on Thursdays. On Fridays, a teacher may choose to give an oral test based on the worksheet questions to allow students to verbally process what they have learned. Please keep in mind that each student will word answers differently, and that is fine. The answers provide you with a guideline.

ALTERNATIVE PLAN: In order to best meet the needs of your schedule, there is an alternative plan as well. If you wish, students will complete the readings on Monday, Tuesday, and Wednesday and also answer 1/3 of the questions provided when they complete the reading. (Students can either write out answers or answer orally.) Projects can be done on Thursdays or Fridays or whenever it best fits your schedule.

AUDIO SELECTIONS: At the end of most chapters, we recommend resources that students will find captivating for spare time, playtime, or travel time. All of the audio books suggested are available at UncleRickAudios.com. For only $10 per month, students will have access to all the suggested audios plus lots more. Each month, they can choose two complete audio books (a $30 value) of their choice. Samples are online to help them make their selections. Uncle Rick makes learning history fun! Publisher's Note: Since the audio selections do concern a time of war, we recommend that all audios be previewed by an adult to determine the age-appropriateness of the material.

STUDENT JOURNAL: Have students set aside a special notebook they will write in after each chapter until they finish the entire history book. He or she should pretend to be a child living during the time of the American War for Independence. The special notebook will be his or her "journal" kept during this time in American history. For each chapter, students should write four sentences describing the events in the chapter as if they happened to him or her or someone in the family.

ADDITIONAL PROJECTS: Throughout this course, students will be introduced to many of our patriotic songs and founding documents. They should take time to memorize them, and it will teach them to be better citizens, learning to be grateful to God for the country He has placed us in. God has blessed America because the Founders based our laws on God's laws. We're not a special people but a blessed people. Many people today have never been taught the history of our country. We pray that God may use each of you to teach others about our godly heritage.

First Semester Suggested Daily Schedule

Week	Day	Assignment	Date/Hours	✓	Grade
		First Semester–First Quarter			
Week 1	Day 1	Ch1 - Why a War of Independence? • Read Pages 7-12: A Heritage of Freedom • *America's Struggle to Become a Nation* • (ASBN) Answer questions 1–5 • Page 17 • *Teacher Guide* • (TG)			
	Day 2	Ch1 - Read Pages 12-15: An Argument with a Proud King • (ASBN) Answer questions 6–10 • Page 17 • (TG)			
	Day 3	Ch1 - Read Pages 15-17: Unjust Laws • (ASBN) Answer questions 11–15 • Page 18 • (TG)			
	Day 4	Choose one of the projects to complete • Page 18 • (TG)			
	Day 5	Ch1 Test • Teacher may give oral exam from worksheet • (TG)			
Week 2	Day 6	Ch2 - Trouble over Taxes • Read Pages 19-22: Furor Over the Stamp Act (ASBN) • Answer questions 1–5 • Page 19 • (TG)			
	Day 7	Ch2 - Read Pages 22-25: More Trouble —Then Violence • (ASBN) Answer questions 6–10 • Pages 19-20 • (TG)			
	Day 8	Ch2 - Read Pages 25-27: The Boston Tea Party • (ASBN) Answer questions 11–15 • Page 20 • (TG)			
	Day 9	Complete the project • Page 20 • (TG)			
	Day 10	Ch2 Test • Teacher may give oral exam from worksheet • (TG)			
Week 3	Day 11	Ch3 - The First Battles • Read Pages 29-31: The First Continental Congress • (ASBN) Answer questions 1–5 • Page 21 • (TG)			
	Day 12	Ch3 - Read Pages 31-33: War Clouds Gather • (ASBN) Answer questions 6–10 • Pages 21-22 • (TG)			
	Day 13	Ch3 - Read Pages 33-35: The Shot Heard 'Round the World (ASBN) • Answer questions 11–15 • Page 22 • (TG)			
	Day 14	Complete the project • Page 22 • (TG)			
	Day 15	Ch3 Test • Teacher may give oral exam from worksheet • (TG)			
Week 4	Day 16	Ch4 - The Choice of a Leader • Read Pages 37-39: America Gets an Army • (ASBN) • Answer questions 1–5 • Page 23 • (TG)			
	Day 17	Ch4 - Read Pages 39-41: Who Will Lead the Army? • (ASBN) Answer questions 6–10 • Pages 23-24 • (TG)			
	Day 18	Ch4 - Read Pages 41-43: A Humble Warrior • (ASBN) Answer questions 11–14 • Page 24 • (TG)			
	Day 19	Complete the project • Page 24 • (TG)			
	Day 20	Ch4 Test • Teacher may give oral exam from worksheet • (TG)			
Week 5	Day 21	Ch5 - Arnold and Allen • Read Pages 45-47: Capture of Ticonderoga • (ASBN) • Answer questions 1–5 • Page 25 • (TG)			
	Day 22	Ch5 - Read Pages 47-50: The Fort Is Taken • (ASBN) Answer questions 6–10 • Pages 25-26 • (TG)			
	Day 23	Ch5 - Read Pages 50-51: America's Most Famous Traitor • (ASBN) Answer questions 11–14 • Page 26 • (TG)			
	Day 24	Choose one of the projects to complete • Page 26 • (TG)			
	Day 25	Ch5 Test • Teacher may give oral exam from worksheet • (TG)			

Week	Day	Assignment	Date/Hours	✓	Grade
Week 6	Day 26	Ch6 - The Battle of Bunker Hill • Read Pages 53-55: Fortifying the Hill • (ASBN) • Answer questions 1–5 • Page 27 • (TG)			
	Day 27	Ch6 - Read Pages 55-57: The Battle Begins • (ASBN) Answer questions 6–10 • Page 27 • (TG)			
	Day 28	Ch6 - Read Pages 57-59: First Blood on the Hill • (ASBN) Answer questions 11–14 • Page 28 • (TG)			
	Day 29	Choose one of the projects to complete • Page 28 • (TG)			
	Day 30	Ch6 Test • Teacher may give oral exam from worksheet • (TG)			
Week 7	Day 31	Ch7 - Life in the New Army • Read Pages 61-63: The General Takes Command • (ASBN) • Answer questions 1–5 • Page 29 • (TG)			
	Day 32	Ch7 - Read Pages 63-65: Life in the Camps • (ASBN) Answer questions 6–10 • Page 29 • (TG)			
	Day 33	Ch7 - Read Pages 66-67: Washington's Leaders • (ASBN) Answer questions 11–15 • Page 30 • (TG)			
	Day 34	Choose one of the projects to complete • Page 30 • (TG)			
	Day 35	Ch7 Test • Teacher may give oral exam from worksheet • (TG)			
Week 8	Day 36	Ch8 - Defeat and Victory in Battle Read Pages 69-71: Some Early Success in Canada • (ASBN) Answer questions 1–5 • Page 31 • (TG)			
	Day 37	Ch8 - Read Pages 71-75: The Quebec Campaign • (ASBN) Answer questions 6–10 • Page 31 • (TG)			
	Day 38	Ch8 - Read Pages 75-77: Taking Back Boston • (ASBN) Answer questions 11–15 • Page 32 • (TG)			
	Day 39	Complete the project • Page 32 • (TG)			
	Day 40	Ch8 Test • Teacher may give oral exam from worksheet • (TG)			
Week 9	Day 41	Ch9 - A Desire for Independence! • Read Pages 79-82: Three Strikes Against King George • (ASBN) • Answer questions 1–5 • Page 33 • (TG)			
	Day 42	Ch9 - Read Pages 82-85: The Declaration of Independence • (ASBN) • Answer questions 6–10 • Pages 33-34 • (TG)			
	Day 43	Ch9 - Read Pages 85-87: The New Nation Celebrates • (ASBN) Answer questions 11–13 • Page 34 • (TG)			
	Day 44	Choose one of the projects to complete • Page 34 • (TG)			
	Day 45	Ch9 Test • Teacher may give oral exam from worksheet • (TG) Optional First Semester–First Quarter Quiz • Pages 87-88 • (TG)			
First Semester–Second Quarter					
Week 1	Day 46	Ch10 - Battles North and South • Read Pages 89-91: Encouragement from the South • (ASBN) Answer questions 1–5 • Page 35 • (TG)			
	Day 47	Ch10 - Read Pages 91-93: The Regulator Movement — First Blood • (ASBN) • Answer questions 6–10 • Page 35 • (TG)			
	Day 48	Ch10 - Read Pages 93-95: The Battle of Sullivan's Island • (ASBN) Answer questions 11–15 • Page 36 • (TG)			
	Day 49	Choose one of the projects to complete • Page 36 • (TG)			
	Day 50	Ch10 Test • Teacher may give oral exam from worksheet • (TG)			

Week	Day	Assignment	Date/Hours	✓	Grade
Week 2	Day 51	Ch11 - Long Island — A Miraculous Escape • Read Pages 97-99: Attempts to End the War — Compromise and Poison • (ASBN) Answer questions 1–5 • Page 37 • (TG)			
	Day 52	Ch11 - Read Pages 99-102: The Battle Takes Shape • (ASBN) Answer questions 6–10 • Pages 37-38 • (TG)			
	Day 53	Ch11 - Read Pages 102-105: Defeat and Retreat • (ASBN) Answer questions 11–15 • Page 38 • (TG)			
	Day 54	Complete the project • Page 38 • (TG)			
	Day 55	Ch11 Test • Teacher may give oral exam from worksheet • (TG)			
Week 3	Day 56	Ch12 - Battles Around New York • Read Pages 107-111: The Retreat from Long Island • (ASBN) Answer questions 1–5 • Page 39 • (TG)			
	Day 57	Ch12 - Read Pages 111-115: Unusual Heroics • (ASBN) Answer questions 6–10 • Page 39 • (TG)			
	Day 58	Ch12 - Read Pages 116-117: Remembrance and Retreat • (ASBN) Answer questions 11–15 • Page 40 • (TG)			
	Day 59	Choose one of the projects to complete • Page 40 • (TG)			
	Day 60	Ch12 Test • Teacher may give oral exam from worksheet • (TG)			
Week 4	Day 61	Ch13 - Retreat and Victory Read Pages 119-122: The Mighty Redcoats Roll On • (ASBN) Answer questions 1–5 • Page 41 • (TG)			
	Day 62	Ch13 - Read Pages 122-125: The Pursued Fox Turns • (ASBN) Answer questions 6–10 • Page 41 • (TG)			
	Day 63	Ch13 - Read Pages 125-127: A Surprise for Cornwallis • (ASBN) Answer questions 11–15 • Page 42 • (TG)			
	Day 64	Choose one of the projects to complete • Page 42 • (TG)			
	Day 65	Ch13 Test • Teacher may give oral exam from worksheet • (TG)			
Week 5	Day 66	Ch14 - The Battle of Valcour Island • Read Pages 129-131: A Tiny Navy • (ASBN) • Answer questions 1–5 • Page 43 • (TG)			
	Day 67	Ch14 - Read Pages 132-133: Another "Benedict Arnold" • (ASBN) Answer questions 6–10 • Pages 43-44 • (TG)			
	Day 68	Ch14 - Read Pages 134-135: Arnold Is Disappointed Again • (ASBN) Answer questions 11–15 • Page 44 • (TG)			
	Day 69	Choose one of the projects to complete • Page 44 • (TG)			
	Day 70	Ch14 Test • Teacher may give oral exam from worksheet • (TG)			
Week 6	Day 71	Ch15 - Burgoyne's Campaign Begins • Read Pages 137-139: High Hopes in Canada, a Reverse in Connecticut • (ASBN) Answer questions 1–5 • Page 45 • (TG)			
	Day 72	Ch15 - Read Pages 140-142: A Confident General Marches to Conquest • (ASBN) • Answer questions 6–10 • Pages 45-46 • (TG)			
	Day 73	Ch15 - Read Pages 142-145: A Surprise Attack • (ASBN) Answer questions 11–15 • Page 46 • (TG)			
	Day 74	Choose one of the projects to complete • Page 46 • (TG)			
	Day 75	Ch15 Test • Teacher may give oral exam from worksheet • (TG)			

Week	Day	Assignment	Date/Hours	✓	Grade
Week 7	Day 76	Ch16 - Bennington and Fort Schuyler Read Pages 147-149: John Stark of New Hampshire • (ASBN) Answer questions 1–5 • Page 47 • (TG)			
	Day 77	Ch16 - Read Pages 149-152: The Siege of Fort Schuyler • (ASBN) Answer questions 6–10 • Pages 47-48 • (TG)			
	Day 78	Ch16 - Read Pages 152-155: A Surprising Victory • (ASBN) Answer questions 11–15 • Page 48 • (TG)			
	Day 79	Choose one of the projects to complete • Page 48 • (TG)			
	Day 80	Ch16 Test • Teacher may give oral exam from worksheet • (TG)			
Week 8	Day 81	Ch17 - The Downfall of Burgoyne • Read Pages 157-159: The Briton Retreats • (ASBN) • Answer questions 1–5 • Page 49 • (TG)			
	Day 82	Ch17 - Read Pages 159-161: A Humiliating End to a Proud Campaign • (ASBN) • Answer questions 6–10 • Pages 49-50 • (TG)			
	Day 83	Ch17 - Read Pages 161-163: Grace to an Enemy • (ASBN) Answer questions 11–15 • Page 50 • (TG)			
	Day 84	Complete the project • Page 50 • (TG)			
	Day 85	Ch17 Test • Teacher may give oral exam from worksheet • (TG)			
Week 9	Day 86	Study day for review or make-up.			
	Day 87	Study day for review or make-up.			
	Day 88	Study day for review or make-up.			
	Day 89	Complete a project from this semester that was not done prior.			
	Day 90	Optional: Give an oral test from the prior worksheets. Optional First Semester–Second Quarter Quiz • Pages 89-90 • (TG)			
		Mid-Term Grade			

Second Semester Suggested Daily Schedule

Week	Day	Assignment	Date/Hours	✓	Grade
		Second Semester–Third Quarter			
Week 1	Day 91	Ch18 - Howe Takes Philadelphia • Read Pages 165-168: Trying to Fool a Fox • (ASBN) • Answer questions 1–5 • Page 51 • (TG)			
	Day 92	Ch18 - Read Pages 168-170: The Fight for Philadelphia • (ASBN) Answer questions 6–10 • Pages 51-52 • (TG)			
	Day 93	Ch18 - Read Pages 170-171: One Winter, Two Armies • (ASBN) Answer questions 11–15 • Page 52 • (TG)			
	Day 94	Complete the project • Page 52 • (TG)			
	Day 95	Ch18 Test • Teacher may give oral exam from worksheet • (TG)			
Week 2	Day 96	Ch19 - A Turning Point in the War Read Pages 173-175: At Last — Help from France • (ASBN) Answer questions 1–5 • Page 53 • (TG)			
	Day 97	Ch19 - Read Pages 175-177: The Race for New York • (ASBN) Answer questions 6–10 • Pages 53-54 • (TG)			
	Day 98	Ch19 - Read Pages 177-179: The Battle of Monmouth • (ASBN) Answer questions 11–15 • Page 54 • (TG)			
	Day 99	Choose one of the projects to complete • Page 54 • (TG)			
	Day 100	Ch19 Test • Teacher may give oral exam from worksheet • (TG)			
Week 3	Day 101	Ch20 - Battles in Various Places • Read Pages 181-183: Fighting East and West • (ASBN) • Answer questions 1–5 • Page 55 • (TG)			
	Day 102	Ch20 - Read Pages 183-185: On the Hudson — The Storming of Stony Point • (ASBN) Answer questions 6–10 • Pages 55-56 • (TG)			
	Day 103	Ch20 - Read Pages 185-187: The Jersey Shore • (ASBN) Answer questions 11 15 • Page 56 • (TG)			
	Day 104	Choose one of the projects to complete • Page 56 • (TG)			
	Day 105	Ch20 Test • Teacher may give oral exam from worksheet • (TG)			
Week 4	Day 106	Ch21 - The Fighting Preacher and Treason • Read Pages 189-193: Minor Engagements, Arnold and Andre • (ASBN) Answer questions 1–5 • Page 57 • (TG)			
	Day 107	Ch21 - Read Pages 193-195: The Treason of Benedict Arnold (ASBN) • Answer questions 6–10 • Pages 57-58 • (TG)			
	Day 108	Ch21 - Read Pages 196-197: Arnold's Escape • (ASBN) Answer questions 11–15 • Page 58 • (TG)			
	Day 109	Choose one of the projects to complete • Page 58 • (TG)			
	Day 110	Ch21 Test • Teacher may give oral exam from worksheet • (TG)			
Week 5	Day 111	Ch22 - Suffering Soldiers • Read Pages 199-201: Suffering in the Camps • (ASBN) • Answer questions 1–5 • Page 59 • (TG)			
	Day 112	Ch22 - Read Pages 201-204: The Mutiny • (ASBN) Answer questions 6–10 • Pages 59-60 • (TG)			
	Day 113	Ch22 - Read Pages 204-209: In the Prisons • (ASBN) Answer questions 11–15 • Page 60 • (TG)			
	Day 114	Choose one of the projects to complete • Page 60 • (TG)			
	Day 115	Ch22 Test • Teacher may give oral exam from worksheet • (TG)			

Week	Day	Assignment	Date/Hours	✓	Grade
Week 6	Day 116	Ch23 - The War in the South • Read Pages 211-214: Militia Battles • (ASBN) • Answer questions 1–5 • Page 61 • (TG)			
	Day 117	Ch23 - Read Pages 214-216: Defending Savannah • (ASBN) Answer questions 6–10 • Pages 61-62 • (TG)			
	Day 118	Ch23 - Read Pages 216-221: The Fall of Charleston, Defeat of Gates and the Battle of King's Mountain • (ASBN) Answer questions 11–15 • Page 62 • (TG)			
	Day 119	Choose one of the projects to complete • Page 62 • (TG)			
	Day 120	Ch23 Test • Teacher may give oral exam from worksheet • (TG)			
Week 7	Day 121	Ch24 - General Greene in the South • Read Pages 223-226: Greene vs. Cornwallis • (ASBN) Answer questions 1–5 • Page 63 • (TG)			
	Day 122	Ch24 - Read Pages 226-228: Victory at Cowpens and the Retreat to Virginia • (ASBN) Answer questions 6–10 • Pages 63-64 • (TG)			
	Day 123	Ch24 - Read Pages 229-231: Greene's Successful Failures • (ASBN) Answer questions 11–15 • Page 64 • (TG)			
	Day 124	Choose one of the projects to complete • Page 64 • (TG)			
	Day 125	Ch24 Test • Teacher may give oral exam from worksheet • (TG)			
Week 8	Day 126	Ch25 - Cornwallis Is Trapped • Read Pages 233-237: Hunting a Traitor • (ASBN) • Answer questions 1–5 • Page 65 • (TG)			
	Day 127	Ch25 - Read Pages 237-240: The Fight Moves to Virginia (ASBN) • Answer questions 6–10 • Page 65 • (TG)			
	Day 128	Ch25 - Read Pages 240-241: Cornwallis in a Corner • (ASBN) Answer questions 11–15 • Page 66 • (TG)			
	Day 129	Choose one of the projects to complete • Page 66 • (TG)			
	Day 130	Ch25 Test • Teacher may give oral exam from worksheet • (TG)			
Week 9	Day 131	Ch26 - Washington Marches South Read Pages 243-245: A Tricky "Old Fox" • (ASBN) Answer questions 1–5 • Page 67 • (TG)			
	Day 132	Ch26 - Read Pages 246-249: The Army Moves at Last • (ASBN) Answer questions 6–10 • Pages 67-68 • (TG)			
	Day 133	Ch26 - Read Pages 249-251: Villainy at New London • (ASBN) Answer questions 11–15 • Page 68 • (TG)			
	Day 134	Complete the project • Page 68 • (TG)			
	Day 135	Ch26 Test • Teacher may give oral exam from worksheet • (TG) Optional Second Semester–Third Quarter Quiz • Pages 91-92 (TG)			
Second Semester–Fourth Quarter					
Week 1	Day 136	Ch27 - Cornwallis Surrenders • Read Pages 253-256: Layfayette Is Loyal and Awaits Orders • (ASBN) Answer questions 1–5 • Page 69 • (TG)			
	Day 137	Ch27 - Read Pages 256-259: Cornwallis Is Embarrassed • (ASBN) Answer questions 6–10 • Pages 69-70 • (TG)			
	Day 138	Ch27 - Read Pages 259-261: Rejoicing in Victory • (ASBN) Answer questions 11–15 • Page 70 • (TG)			
	Day 139	Choose one of the projects to complete • Page 70 • (TG)			
	Day 140	Ch27 Test • Teacher may give oral exam from worksheet • (TG)			

Week	Day	Assignment	Date/Hours	✓	Grade
Week 2	Day 141	Ch28 - A Strange War on the Sea • Read Pages 263-265: The Struggle for a Navy • (ASBN) Answer questions 1–5 • Page 71 • (TG)			
	Day 142	Ch28 - Read Pages 265-268: Jones Terrorizes the British Coast (ASBN) • Answer questions 6–10 • Pages 71-72 • (TG)			
	Day 143	Ch28 - Read Pages 268-269: The Nation Thanks John Paul Jones • (ASBN) • Answer questions 11–15 • Page 72 • (TG)			
	Day 144	Complete the project • Page 72 • (TG)			
	Day 145	Ch28 Test • Teacher may give oral exam from worksheet • (TG)			
Week 3	Day 146	Ch29 - War in the West • Read Pages 271-273: Redcoats and Indians in the Ohio Country • (ASBN) Answer questions 1–5 • Page 73 • (TG)			
	Day 147	Ch29 - Read Pages 273-275: Increasing Bloodshed in the West (ASBN) • Answer questions 6–10 • Pages 73-74 • (TG)			
	Day 148	Ch29 - Read Pages 275-277: George Rogers Clark Illinois Campain • (ASBN) • Answer questions 11–15 • Page 74 • (TG)			
	Day 149	Complete the project • Page 74 • (TG)			
	Day 150	Ch29 Test • Teacher may give oral exam from worksheet • (TG)			
Week 4	Day 151	Ch30 - An Unsettled Peace • Read Pages 279-282: The Dust of War Settles • (ASBN) • Answer questions 1–5 • Page 75 • (TG)			
	Day 152	Ch30 - Read Pages 282-284: Problems with the Army • (ASBN) Answer questions 6–10 • Pages 75-76 • (TG)			
	Day 153	Ch30 - Read Pages 284-287: The General Says Good-bye • (ASBN) Answer questions 11–15 • Page 76 • (TG)			
	Day 154	Choose one of the projects to complete • Page 76 • (TG)			
	Day 155	Ch30 Test • Teacher may give oral exam from worksheet • (TG)			
Week 5	Day 156	Ch31 - The United States Constitution • Read Pages 289-294: A New Form of Government • (ASBN) Answer questions 1–5 • Page 77 • (TG)			
	Day 157	Ch31 - Read Pages 295-298: A New Constitutional Republic (ASBN) • Answer questions 6–10 • Pages 77-78 • (TG)			
	Day 158	Ch31 - Read Pages 298-305: How the Constitution Works (ASBN) • Answer questions 11–15 • Page 78 • (TG)			
	Day 159	Complete the project • Page 78 • (TG)			
	Day 160	Ch31 Test • Teacher may give oral exam from worksheet • (TG)			
Week 6	Day 161	Ch32 - The New Republic • Read Pages 307-309: Early Times in the New Nation • (ASBN) Answer questions 1–5 • Page 79 • (TG)			
	Day 162	Ch32 - Read Pages 310-313: Early Development, Regional Differences • (ASBN) Answer questions 6–10 • Pages 79-80 • (TG)			
	Day 163	Ch32 - Read Pages 313-315: Washington's Presidency • (ASBN) Answer questions 11–15 • Page 80 • (TG)			
	Day 164	Complete the project • Page 80 • (TG)			
	Day 165	Ch32 Test • Teacher may give oral exam from worksheet • (TG)			

Week	Day	Assignment	Date/Hours	✓	Grade
Week 7	Day 166	Ch33 - Who Were the Signers of the Declaration of Independence? • Read Pages 317-321 to New Jersey Answer questions 1–5 • Page 81 • (TG)			
	Day 167	Ch33 - Read Pages 321-325 to Georgia • (ASBN) Answer questions 6–10 • Pages 81-82 • (TG)			
	Day 168	Ch33 - Read Pages 325-332 • (ASBN) Answer questions 11–14 • Page 82 • (TG)			
	Day 169	Complete the project • Page 82 • (TG)			
	Day 170	Ch33 Test • Teacher may give oral exam from worksheet • (TG)			
Week 8	Day 171	Ch34 - Who Were the Signers of the Constitution? Read Pages 335-339 to New Jersey • (ASBN) Answer questions 1–5 • Page 83 • (TG)			
	Day 172	Ch34 - Read Pages 339-341 to Massachusetts • (ASBN) Answer questions 6–10 • Pages 83-84 • (TG)			
	Day 173	Ch34 - Read Pages 341-346 • (ASBN) Answer questions 11–15 • Page 84 • (TG)			
	Day 174	Complete the project • Page 84 • (TG)			
	Day 175	Ch34 Test • Teacher may give oral exam from worksheet • (TG)			
Week 9	Day 176	Study day for quiz.			
	Day 177	Study day for quiz.			
	Day 178	Study day for quiz.			
	Day 179	Complete a project from this semester that was not done prior.			
	Day 180	Optional Bonus Quiz: Who Am I? • Pages 95-100 • (TG) Optional Second Semester–Fourth Quarter Quiz • Pages 93-94 (TG)			
		Final Grade			

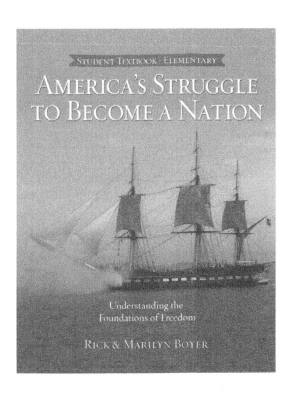

History Worksheets

for Use with

America's Struggle to Become a Nation

Questions

1. Did the colonists consider themselves Americans or Englishmen?

2. Did the colonists and the people in England have much in common?

3. What was the name of the great revival that swept the colonies before the War of Independence?

4. Who were the Puritans?

5. How does the gospel teach us that kings are no better than other men?

6. Were the American colonies developing a culture of their own that was distinct from English culture?

7. What did "taxation without representation" mean?

8. Why was England deep in debt?

9. How many men did Benjamin Franklin say the colonies had provided for the French and Indian War?

10. Was King George a wise and humble king?

11. What did the Navigation Acts require?

12. Were the Navigation Acts firmly enforced when they were first made law?

13. What did the Iron Act of 1750 forbid?

14. Why were the Navigation Acts and the Iron Act not strictly enforced in the early days?

15. Why did the king send soldiers to America?

Projects for Chapter 1

1. Journal Entry: Write about your parents' reaction to having to pay extra money when they bought an almanac because the almanac had to have a British stamp on it. Write about what it was like to see British soldiers in your town. Were you surprised? Were your dad and mom happy to see them? Or upset? Why?

2. Pretend you are one of King George III's servants. You have an uncle and aunt living in America. Write a letter to them, describing the king's angry reaction to the American colonies. Did he slam his fist on his throne? Did he yell? If so, what did he yell? Tell your uncle and aunt what you think of the taxes, the closing of the Boston ports, and the declaration of American lands to suddenly belong to Quebec. Use at least six sentences.

   1.

   2.

   3.

   4.

   5.

   6.

Questions

1. Did most American colonists want independence from England when they heard of the Stamp Act?

2. What patriot made the famous "Give Me Liberty or Give Me Death" speech?

3. Why did many of the stamp tax collectors quickly quit their jobs?

4. Why did English merchants object to the Stamp Act?

5. How long was the Stamp Act in effect?

6. What were the people called who believed the king had a right to do as he wished with the colonies?

7. What did the colonists realize the king was trying to do by replacing the Stamp Act with a new tax on tea, paint, lead, and glass?

8. Why did the British seize the *Liberty*, John Hancock's ship?

9. Who defended the British soldiers of the Boston Massacre in court?

10. What British revenue ship was burned by men from Rhode Island?

11. Why did the king think the colonists would start drinking tea again after he took off the other taxes and lowered the price of tea?

12. What did patriots in Philadelphia and New York do with the tea that was shipped into their harbors?

13. How did the patriots who dumped the tea disguise themselves?

14. Was the Boston Tea Party a violent riot?

15. What was the value of the tea that was dumped in Boston Harbor?

Project for Chapter 2

1. Journal Entry: Pretend your uncle went on board the *Dartmouth* to help destroy the tea. What did he use to blacken his face? How many tea chests did he break open and throw into the sea? Did the crewmen of the ship try to stop him? Or did they know they should not fight and just watch? How did this make you feel about him? Were you embarrassed or proud of him?

Questions

1. What did the Boston Port Bill prohibit?

2. How did the Massachusetts Bill change the government in Massachusetts?

3. What was the Quebec Bill?

4. Why didn't Georgia send delegates to the First Continental Congress?

5. Who went to England to try to speak to Parliament on behalf of Congress?

6. What was General Howe's attitude toward war with the colonies?

7. Whom did the king send to lead the royal navy in America?

8. Who were the Minutemen?

9. Did the British leaders respect the Minutemen as a fighting force?

10. Why did General Gage send a force to Concord?

11. Who was another rider who left Boston for Concord with Paul Revere?

12. Why did the two men leave Boston by different routes?

13. What two patriot leaders were spending the night in Lexington?

14. Why were the British not successful in seizing large amounts of war material at Concord?

15. Why did the Minutemen already have some fighting experience?

Project for Chapter 3

1. Journal Entry: Pretend your uncle and oldest cousins helped to move supplies to hide them from the British raiders. What did they move? Did they work at night? How did they disguise what they were doing? Pretend one of your cousins took part in the fighting. Did he get shot? Did he shoot any British soldiers? If so, how many?

Questions

1. What was the response from the other colonies when news spread of the fighting in Massachusetts?

2. What two important events happened on May 10, 1775?

3. Who was voted to be the president of the Congress?

4. What did John Adams think Congress should do about the army of men who had gathered around Boston to hold the British in?

5. What did Adams predict would happen if Congress failed to adopt the army?

6. Why did John Adams suggest the appointment of a southerner for general of the army?

7. Who was the commander of the army when Congress began debating about the army?

8. Did John Adams agree with his cousin Sam's praise of Ward?

9. Did Washington expect to be chosen as commander of the army?

10. Did Congress approve Adams' suggestion?

11. Was Washington confident in his abilities as a general?

12. How much was Washington to be paid as a general in the army?

13. What was Washington's pet nickname for his wife, Martha?

14. Where did Washington go as soon as he left Congress?

Project for Chapter 4

1. Journal Entry: Pretend a relative was at the meeting of the Continental Congress, and he wrote a letter to you describing what happened. He wrote of John Adams speaking of what the new Continental Army needed in a leader, and of the surprise on George Washington's face when John Adams nominated him. Also write about your neighbor, who left his farm to travel to Massachusetts to help fight. How many children did your neighbor have? Were they afraid for their dad? Or were they excited?

Questions

1. How did General Amherst succeed in taking Ticonderoga from the French after General Abercrombie had failed?

2. On what lake was Ticonderoga located?

3. Who was the British commander of Fort Ticonderoga in 1775?

4. Why did Arnold suggest taking the fort?

5. Who guided Allen in his conquest of the fort?

6. In whose name did Ethan Allen claim Fort Ticonderoga?

7. What additional fort did the Green Mountain Boys take on May 12?

8. What did Benedict Arnold try to do when Fort Ticonderoga was captured?

9. What fort did Arnold and his men capture shortly after Ticonderoga was taken?

10. What did the Congress plan to do with the military supplies captured at Ticonderoga if peace was restored between the Americans and the British?

11. What made the Arnold family's financial problems even worse?

12. Why was young Benedict Arnold taken out of school?

13. How did Arnold learn the business of apothecary?

14. How did Arnold get his first military experience?

Projects for Chapter 5

1. Journal Entry: Pretend your brother has gone up with Ethan Allen and imagine how you felt when he left. Soon you receive a letter back from him, telling of what happened. What did he think of Benedict Arnold? What did he think of Ethan Allen and their victory?

2. Read the words of "My Country 'Tis of Thee" and the story behind the song on page 94. Count the times it references God. Learn the song. If you can play an instrument, learn to play it.

Questions

1. Did the patriots from Massachusetts get help from the other colonies in the siege of Boston?

2. What did New Jersey do with the money in their colonial treasury?

3. What did the Mecklenburg Declaration of Independence state that the colony of North Carolina had the right to do?

4. What did General Gage's proclamation offer to the colonists?

5. Did the proclamation of General Gage cause the patriots to give up and lay down their arms?

6. Who was in command of the patriots on Breed's Hill?

7. What happened in Cambridge where the troops gathered before marching to Bunker Hill?

8. Why did the patriots fortify Breed's Hill instead of Bunker Hill?

9. Were the British surprised to see fortifications on Breed's Hill?

10. Why did the British want to drive the patriots off Breed's Hill?

11. How many redcoats landed to charge Breed's Hill?

12. Did the redcoats expect the patriots to put up a strong fight?

13. What was the British soldiers' reaction to the first volley from the patriots?

14. Why did the patriots retreat after the third charge from the British?

Projects for Chapter 6

1. Journal Entry: Pretend you knew one of the men who died fighting on Breed's Hill. Write about your sadness that he died and about his bravery. How many British soldiers was he able to shoot down? How long the night before had he stayed up to help build the fort?

2. Activity — Make your own fort

   You will need:

   - 4 cups of flour

   - 1½ cups of salt

   - 2 cups of water

   - 1 tablespoon oil

   - green food coloring (optional)

   - 2 packages of M&M® candies

   Mix the first four ingredients. You will use this dough to make a "hill" and a fort. If you want, add green food coloring to a part of the dough for your "hill." You can shape the dough around an upturned bowl to make the hill shape. Form the fort on the hill with the uncolored dough. Using only red candies, place "Redcoats" around the fort, marching in formation. Using other colors, put "American militia men" inside the fort. Option: Make the fort out of cookie dough and eat it when you are done.

   Be sure to use an oven-proof bowl. Bake at 250 degrees for two hours, checking for doneness. Carefully remove the bowl from beneath the hill.

Questions

1. What British official arrived in New York on the same day as Washington?

2. What encouraging news reached Washington at New York on his way to Cambridge?

3. What did Washington's council of war decide was the first order of business?

4. Name three things forbidden by Washington's general orders of July 4, 1775.

5. What did the orders require of all officers and men not on actual duty?

6. How did Washington provide for his men to live and fight alongside their friends and neighbors?

7. At what time of day were orders read to the soldiers?

8. Which colony had the most men in camp at Cambridge?

9. Who was William Emerson?

10. Did all the soldiers live in tents?

11. Which soldiers were said to be able to load their rifles while running through the woods?

12. What words of Patrick Henry did Morgan's men have written on their hunting shirts?

13. What was the nickname of General Nathanael Greene?

14. Which general had been wounded 15 times in the French and Indian War?

15. Which general hoped to replace Washington as commander of the army?

Projects for Chapter 7

1. Journal Entry: Pretend you have read newspaper accounts of American army camp life. Write what you thought of the variety of the tents and all the folks from every colony living together. Write about sending a package to your cousin who is in one of the army camps. What did you send him? Did you make anything that was sent — knitted socks, treats, or a card?

2. Design your own flag. Your flag should express your unwillingness to submit to the king, and/or your pride in America. You may also include a symbol of Christianity. Some symbols you might use would be: a bald eagle, a snake, a crown (of King George III or of God), a cross, a soldier, a woman (often used to symbolize justice). What colors will your flag have? Draw your flag on a 4 x 6 card, using up the entire card. (You can put the card over another sheet of paper, so you can color all the way to the edge of the card.)

Questions

1. Why did Benedict Arnold resign his commission?

2. Was Arnold a brave fighter?

3. What two leaders wrote to Congress suggesting an invasion of Canada?

4. Why did Montgomery replace Schuyler in command?

5. What two forts did Montgomery capture before moving on to Montreal?

6. When had Montgomery fought against Quebec before?

7. How long did it take for Arnold to march to Quebec?

8. What was the response when the Americans demanded that the British surrender or come out and fight?

9. What famous American officer fought his way into the city and got captured?

10. What disease killed many men in the American camp before spring?

11. How far did Colonel Henry Knox move the cannons from Ticonderoga to Boston?

12. Why was the location of Dorchester Heights important to the two armies?

13. Why did Washington fire his cannons on two nights before the advance on Dorchester Heights?

14. What did General Howe say about the sudden appearance of fortifications on Dorchester Heights?

15. Why did Washington not fire on the British as they left Boston?

Project for Chapter 8

1. Journal Entry: Pretend you have read a newspaper account of Montgomery and Benedict Arnold's defeat at Montreal. What do you think of it? What do you think of Benedict Arnold?

   Also, pretend you received a thank-you note from your cousin in the army camp. What did the note say, and what did your cousin like best in his package?

Questions

1. Why did Congress send the Olive Branch Petition to the king and Parliament?

2. Were the patriots really in rebellion against lawful authority?

3. What document did King George publish after Congress sent the Olive Branch Petition?

4. What did the British Captain Mowat do to the town of Falmouth, Maine?

5. What did King George do to get more soldiers to fight against America?

6. Which colony was the first to instruct its representatives to vote for independence?

7. Who made the first resolution urging a Declaration of Independence?

8. Who seconded Lee's motion?

9. Why was Richard Henry Lee not on the committee to draft the Declaration?

10. Who signed the Declaration of Independence on July 4, 1776?

11. Why was George Washington in New York?

12. What happened to the lead from the statue of King George that was pulled down by the patriots?

13. Which signer of the Declaration helped to make bullets out of pieces of the statue?

Projects for Chapter 9

1. Journal Entry: America has declared independence! Write about the celebrations that went on in your town. Were you able to go to the public reading of the Declaration of Independence? What did you think of it? What did your father and mother do? What did they say about it afterward?

   In your neatest handwriting, copy the first two sentences of the Declaration of Independence. Below, rewrite each phrase in your own words. If necessary, ask your teacher to separate the sentences into phrases for you.

2. Document Memorization: Learn the Preamble to the Declaration of Independence. If you want to read the whole thing, you'll find it in the appendix of the textbook (page 349). Practice it each day for just a few minutes until you can say it word perfect.

Questions

1. What is the definition of a state?

2. Who set the taxes for the people of the new states?

3. What encouraged the patriots that they could, in fact, win their independence?

4. What British general invaded North Carolina in 1776?

5. Why did the patriots fight the Tories at Moore's Creek Bridge?

6. Who were the Regulators?

7. Why did the Regulators resist the government?

8. What building project made North Carolinians feel that Governor Tryon was corrupt?

9. What group did Tryon send to fight against the Regulators?

10. Who was Edmund Fanning?

11. What city were the patriots in Fort Moultrie defending?

12. Who was in charge of Fort Moultrie?

13. Why did cannonballs do little damage to the fort's walls?

14. What American officer predicted that Fort Moultrie's walls would not stand under bombardment?

15. Why could Clinton's soldiers not wade across the channel and attack Fort Moultrie?

Projects for Chapter 10

1. Journal Entry: Pretend you know someone who used to be a Regulator in North Carolina. Write about how this person united with the patriots against the king. Write about how this person had been unfairly treated by the corrupt government. Was his land taxed too much? Did the sheriff destroy the record of his tax payments?

2. Read the words of the "Star Spangled Banner" and the story behind the writing of it on page 95. Learn to sing it and be sure to learn ALL the verses. Pay close attention to the last verse and notice the references to God and praise given to God for our freedom. If you play an instrument, learn to play it. Maybe you and your family or friends could even sing it together. Out of respect for our country, you should place your right hand over your heart whenever you hear this song being sung, as this is our country's national anthem.

   Think of what it would have been like to be Francis Scott Key, straining to see if the flag was still waving. I think of this every time I sing the song.

Questions

1. Where did the British sail to after being beaten in Boston?

2. Why did the British expect to have an easier time in New York than in New England?

3. What did General Howe hope to do rather than attacking Washington?

4. Where was Governor Tryon before the battle of Long Island?

5. How many people were suspected of being involved in the Tory plot that included poisoning General Washington?

6. What was Washington doing while Howe was trying to make peace?

7. What capable general did Washington put in charge of defenses on Long Island?

8. Why did Greene not remain in command?

9. Why did Washington not take over the Long Island defenses himself?

10. What did the patriots do to try to keep the British from sending their ships upriver?

11. Which officer led the largest company of British soldiers on Long Island?

12. Why was General Sullivan's position so unfavorable?

13. Why did General Stirling's men have so much trouble getting across Gowanus Creek?

14. Why could Howe's ships not go up the river fast enough to cut off the patriots' escape from Long Island?

15. Why did the British not see Washington's men being rowed to safety after the sun came up?

Project for Chapter 11

1. Journal Entry: Pretend your cousin in the army camp was involved in the defeat in New York. What did he see? Did he get wounded? How does he feel, having lost this battle?

Questions

1. What decision was made in Washington's council of war on Long Island?

2. How did General Mifflin fool the British into believing that Washington's army was still in camp?

3. Did Washington succeed in getting all his men off the island by daybreak?

4. What providential occurrence prevented the British from seeing the last of Washington's men escape in boats?

5. Whom did General Howe send to Congress with an offer of pardon?

6. What was the *Turtle*?

7. What ship did the *Turtle* attempt to blow up?

8. Why was the *Turtle* unsuccessful?

9. What success did Lee later have in attacking British vessels?

10. What patriot soldier spied on the British on Long Island and was hanged when caught?

11. Were the patriot soldiers in New York intimidated by the large and better-equipped British army?

12. Was Washington successful in rallying those men to fight?

13. Who was the patriot lady who delayed Howe with a lunch invitation, allowing Putnam's army to escape?

14. Why did the British not settle down and spend the winter in New York as expected?

15. How did an ingenious American soldier survive hiding from the Tories under a pile of ashes?

Projects for Chapter 12

1. Journal Entry: Pretend you have read about Nathan Hale's execution in the newspaper. What did you think of it? What did you think of his letters being destroyed by William Cunningham, and Cunningham's refusal to allow Nathan Hale a visit from a pastor, or a Bible? What are your thoughts now about the future of the war?

2. Draw a diagram of what you think Bushnell's "marine turtle" looked like. Remember, it was 10 feet long and 6 feet wide. How would Ezra Lee have fit inside it? Where are the cranks located inside, and the paddles outside? What about the hand pump? What did the mechanism that would screw the torpedo onto the ship look like?

Questions

1. Who was the American commander of Fort Washington?

2. How many Americans were lost in the fall of Fort Washington?

3. What general evacuated Fort Lee?

4. What helpful things did the British capture at Fort Lee?

5. What did General Howe do to try to persuade the colonists to return to loyalty to the king?

6. What American general was captured near Morristown?

7. What did Cornwallis, confident of victory, decide to do at this time?

8. Who rowed the army across the icy Delaware River?

9. What were conditions like for General Washington's army as they marched toward Trenton?

10. How many Hessian prisoners were taken at Princeton?

11. What slowed the British troops down more than General Greene's small force of men?

12. How did Washington fool Cornwallis into believing that his army was still in camp across the Assunpink?

13. How many men did the British lose at Princeton in killed, wounded, and captured?

14. What delayed Cornwallis on his march to Princeton?

15. Did Cornwallis attack the Continental army at Princeton?

Projects for Chapter 13

1. Journal Entry: Pretend your cousin was involved in at least one of these successes: defeating the Hessians in Trenton after Christmas feasting or defeating the British at Princeton. What did your cousin do? Did he kill any British or Hessian soldiers? Did he get injured? What did he think of Washington's orders, when so many soldiers were so tired and didn't even have shoes?

2. Learn the Pledge of Allegiance. Remember to place your right hand over your heart when reciting the pledge and look at the flag if one is available.

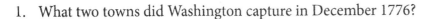
Questions

1. What two towns did Washington capture in December 1776?

2. Why did the British want to control a waterway from Quebec to New York?

3. Where did Arnold get his ships?

4. How long did the fighting last on the first day of the battle?

5. Which American ship surrendered?

6. What general was impressed with the courage of Bettys in the Battle of Valcour Island?

7. What happened in Canada after Bettys was captured that ended up costing him his life?

8. Why was Bettys not hung the first time he was caught spying?

9. Why could Bettys not fire his musket when he was captured?

10. What did Bettys attempt to burn when he was captured?

11. What fort did Arnold decide was the most important fort to hold?

12. Why did Carleton say he did not stay on Lake Champlain to attack Ticonderoga?

13. Was Benedict Arnold rewarded for his bravery in the Battle of Valcour Island?

14. Why was Arnold not promoted at this time?

15. Why did Arnold not resign from the army as he had threatened?

Projects for Chapter 14

1. Journal Entry: Pretend you have read about Benedict Arnold's success on Lake Champlain. What do you think of him? What did you think of America's chances of winning the war, when you read how brave he was? Also, you have read about Joe Bettys' treachery. What do you think of him? What kind of punishment do you think he deserves? Why do you think he became a traitor?

2. Read *America the Beautiful* and the story behind it on page 99, and then draw a picture of the place you find most beautiful.

Questions

1. What boastful saying of Burgoyne's was well known?

2. What British officer was to lead his force to meet Burgoyne in Albany?

3. Why did British officer William Tryon raid Danbury, Connecticut?

4. What did Tryon do to Danbury besides taking the supplies?

5. What American officer rode from New Haven to help the militia fight Tryon's force?

6. What nickname did Burgoyne get because of his taste for expensive things?

7. How many men were in Burgoyne's force?

8. How many men did General St. Clair have to defend Fort Ticonderoga?

9. How did the British discover St. Clair's night evacuation of the fort?

10. What two officers did St. Clair leave at Hubbardton as a rear guard?

11. Why did Colonel Warner's men retreat after having driven their British pursuers back at first?

12. Where did St. Clair finally join Schuyler?

13. What did John Adams say America must do to be able to hold her posts?

14. What did the retreating Americans do to slow the advance of Burgoyne?

15. What Hessian officer attacked the patriots at Bennington to get supplies for Burgoyne?

Projects for Chapter 15

1. Journal Entry: Pretend you have heard of Burgoyne's advances from a soldier who had to retreat. What did the soldier tell you? Was he himself injured? What do you think of the Indians helping General Burgoyne? (Remember that the Indians were especially cruel.) What do you think of Burgoyne's willingness to let Indians treat Americans this way?

2. Go on a scavenger hunt for people. Fold a sheet of paper in half. On one side, write "British" at the top, and on the other side, write "American." Find all these people, and write their names on their side of the paper, according to if they are British or American: General John Burgoyne, Carleton, Colonel Barry St. Leger, General Clinton, William Tryon, Benedict Arnold, General Philip Schuyler, General Gates, General Reidesel, General Frazer, General St. Clair, General Philips, Colonel Watner, Colonel Francis, Colonel Baum, Breyman.

   Pick three people on each side and write one or two sentences about what they did in this chapter.

Questions

1. What did Washington ask John Stark to do after the battle at Princeton?

2. Why did Stark resign from the Continental army?

3. Why did the militiamen from Massachusetts complain?

4. What did John Stark promise the Massachusetts militia?

5. Why did the Hessians mistake the militiamen for Tories?

6. What was the monumental task Stark's men faced?

7. Who came to the rescue of the tired Yankees after their victory on the hill?

8. What were the concerns of the discouraged Burgoyne?

9. What did the British colonel Leger use to carry his men into the Mohawk Valley?

10. What did God command Joshua and His people as recorded in Joshua 1:9?

11. What Tory helped to break the siege of Fort Schuyler?

12. What was he ordered to do by Benedict Arnold?

13. How did Arnold make sure that Schuyler would fulfill his mission?

14. What did Hanyost show the Indians to prove he had been shot at while escaping?

15. Whose idea was this trick?

Projects for Chapter 16

1. Journal Entry: Pretend you have read about the victory over the Hessians and Burgoyne near Bennington. Make a note of it in your journal. Pretend your cousin was trapped in the siege at Fort Schuyler and wrote you a letter about it. What did he say about his surprise when the British army and the Indians left? Was he himself able to eat any of the food the retreating soldiers left behind? If so, what did he eat, and what other things did his friends find?

2. Begin to memorize the Preamble to the Constitution. We need to become familiar with the law of our land. You are one of "We the People," and God holds you responsible to know what the Constitution says. We are all to be guardians of the freedom passed on to us by the Founders.

Questions

1. Who led the sharpshooters who did so much damage to Burgoyne's army?

2. Which two officers had a jealous relationship?

3. Which Polish officer put his engineering skills to work for the American army?

4. Which officer was most responsible for the victory at Freeman's farm?

5. Who got the most credit for the victory in Gates' report of the battle?

6. Which general was coming from New York to help Burgoyne?

7. In what part of the body was Arnold wounded for the second time?

8. Which officer's wife burned her own wheat fields?

9. How did General Clinton try to get a message to General Burgoyne?

10. Why did Gates not insist on an unconditional surrender from Burgoyne?

11. What was the Conway Cabal?

12. Where did Burgoyne and his party stay on their way to Boston as prisoners?

13. What kind of reception did Schuyler's family give them?

14. How did Madame de Riedesel say the prisoners were treated by the Schuylers?

15. What was the effect of the murder of Jane McCrea on the patriot militia?

Project for Chapter 17

1. Journal Entry: Pretend you have heard of Benedict Arnold's successes from your cousin. Write about your confusion when you read in the paper that General Gates was given all the credit for the surrender of Burgoyne. Which account do you think is true? Why? Also, what do you think of Mrs. Shuyler's generosity and kindness to Burgoyne?

Questions

1. What city did General Howe especially want to capture?

2. Whom did Howe leave in charge of New York while he moved across New Jersey toward Philadelphia?

3. How did General Howe use ships to try to confuse Washington?

4. Why did Washington not march his army south when it appeared that Howe was headed toward Charleston?

5. How many men did the Americans lose at Brandywine?

6. What good was accomplished by Washington at Brandywine and through the harassment of Howe's army on the way to Philadelphia?

7. How did General Howe find out about Mad Anthony Wayne's camp?

8. Why was General Gray called the "no-flint" general?

9. What two forts near Philadelphia posed a threat to Howe?

10. What was the last major battle for Washington before winter?

11. Did the redcoats have a difficult winter in Philadelphia?

12. Where did the patriots encamp for the winter?

13. What German officer helped Washington by intensely training the soldiers in military skill?

14. What patriot woman from Philadelphia disguised herself as a market woman to take food and medicine to the patriots in Valley Forge?

15. How did Mary once hide her officer brother from the redcoats?

Project for Chapter 18

1. Journal Entry: What did your cousin, who was at Valley Forge over the terrible winter, think of the horrible conditions?

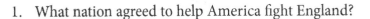
Questions

1. What nation agreed to help America fight England?

2. Whom did America send to France to try to get help?

3. What did England do to try to end the war after hearing that France was going to help the colonies?

4. What admiral led the French fleet to America?

5. What British general's defeat encouraged France to believe that America could win the war?

6. Why did the British decide to leave Philadelphia and return to New York?

7. Why were the Tories eager to leave Philadelphia?

8. How did Clinton arrange transportation for the Tories who wanted to flee to New York?

9. How many Tories were punished for helping the British in Philadelphia?

10. What did the Continental Congress do when the British departed?

11. What action did Washington propose to do in order to catch up with Clinton?

12. Where was Clinton finally caught and engaged in battle?

13. What was the weather like on the day of battle?

14. For how long was Charles Lee dismissed from the army for ordering an unnecessary retreat?

15. Who was Molly Pitcher?

Projects for Chapter 19

1. Do some research on the area of Valley Forge at the time of the Revolutionary War and draw a map of the significant cities, states, battlefields, and rivers in the area.

2. Write a poem or song of your own about Molly Pitcher and her bravery in battle.

Questions

1. How did Washington hope to end the war without attacking the British in New York?

2. Why did the French fleet not attack New York?

3. How did the French fleet help Washington by leaving for the West Indies?

4. Who attacked patriot settlements in the Wyoming Valley?

5. What general was sent west to quiet the Indians?

6. What general led the attack on Stony Point?

7. On what important river was Stony Point located?

8. Why did most of Wayne's men not have their guns loaded?

9. What did Wayne order his men to do when he was wounded?

10. How did Washington want British prisoners to be treated by his men?

11. Who is sometimes called the Father of the American Navy?

12. Who were the privateers?

13. What was a privateer's license called?

14. Who was a privateer who lived in New Brunswick, New Jersey, and had formerly served in the British navy?

15. Why did Hyler not destroy all five of the ships he captured in one fight?

Projects for Chapter 20

1. Journal Entry: Pretend your cousin received the supplies you sent him. Did he share any of the things with his friends? Did your cousin go with General Sullivan to fight the Indians and the Tories? Write about whether or not he went and what he thought of the venture. If he went, write about what he did and saw. If he stayed behind, write about his helping to take Stony Point Fort with Mad Anthony Wayne.

2. Learn your States and Capitals: During this school year, you need to learn the states and capitals of the United States. You can practice learning them each day until you learn them all. It just takes a few minutes a day and soon you will know them all. Sometimes it's fun to do a United States puzzle that has states and the capitals on it.

Questions

1. Who was the Revolutionary War general whose son would be the top general in the Confederate army?

2. What reward did Congress give Lee for his attack on Paulus Hook?

3. What preacher was nicknamed the Fighting Chaplain?

4. What did Caldwell keep on his pulpit when preaching in case of trouble?

5. What outrage did the Hessians commit against Caldwell?

6. What military disaster happened to the patriots in May of 1780?

7. How did the British make colonial money worth much less than it was at first?

8. Why was Benedict Arnold under financial pressure?

9. What important fort did he agree to turn over to the British?

10. Who was the British officer carrying messages between Arnold and General Clinton?

11. What was Benedict Arnold doing when he learned that he was about to be exposed as a spy?

12. How did he make his escape?

13. On what British ship did Arnold take refuge?

14. What did John Andre beg General Washington to do?

15. What happened when Peggy Arnold tried to return to her family in Philadelphia?

Projects for Chapter 21

1. Journal Entry: Pretend you have read about the murders of Mrs. Caldwell and the Rev. Caldwell in the paper. What do you think of this? What do you think of their children? Pretend you have read of Benedict Arnold's treachery. Write what you think of him.

2. Pick your favorite stanza from the poem on pages 192–193 of your textbook. Draw a picture to illustrate what the words describe. If you cannot depict the stanza in one picture, draw two. Copy the stanza beneath your picture(s).

Questions

1. Why was there little fighting in the north during 1781?

2. Were the American soldiers paid regularly?

3. How long did Washington say that his men were sometimes without bread?

4. What did the local farmers complain to Washington about?

5. What two officers' wives were known for trying to make camp life easier for the men?

6. What part of the army mutinied on January 1, 1781?

7. What was the British response when they heard of the mutiny?

8. Besides the complaints of the rest of the army, what other problem did the Pennsylvania men suffer?

9. What did the mutineers plan to do about their complaints?

10. What did General Wayne to do keep the men from stealing from farmers along the march?

11. What does it mean to "parole" a prisoner?

12. How did Washington tell his men to treat prisoners?

13. Why did the British soldiers not treat their prisoners with the respect due to prisoners of war?

14. What were the worst prisons the British had?

15. What did the British require the prisoners to do in order to be released?

Projects for Chapter 22

1. Journal Entry: Pretend your cousin has written you a letter, telling you of his struggles in the army camp. What did he write to you? Your family has suffered from the war as well, and you do not have much to send him in another package. What will you send him? Pretend you have read an account from a prisoner who escaped from the British prisoner ship, the *Jersey*. What do you think of the prisoner's struggles, compared to your cousin's?

2. States and Capitals: Practice learning states and capitals.

Questions

1. Why did the British turn their attention to the southern colonies late in the war?

2. What did the British hope would result in the south, even if they lost the war?

3. What town did the Tories destroy on their way home from the unsuccessful expedition against Sunbury?

4. Who was the American commander in Georgia?

5. Who helped the British find a way to get behind Howe's force at Savannah?

6. What officer was placed in charge of the patriot army in the south after the fall of Savannah?

7. What commander defeated the British attack at Port Royal Island?

8. How many Americans survived the battle of Brier Creek and returned to join Lincoln?

9. What event encouraged the Americans and led to their attack on Savannah?

10. What famous Polish officer fell in the October 4, 1779, attempt to recapture Savannah?

11. Who were the commanding generals at the siege of Charleston?

12. What was meant by "Tarleton's quarter" after the Battle of Waxhaw's?

13. Who was defeated at the Battle of Camden, South Carolina?

14. Why did Cornwallis not follow up his victory at Camden with another major battle?

15. In what battle was Major Ferguson defeated and killed?

Projects for Chapter 23

1. Journal Entry: Pretend you have heard about the new British tactic of fighting in the south and of America's many defeats. Write what you thought of this. What do you think of the Tories committing crimes across the countryside? Write whether or not you think America will win the war. Pretend you have heard of the battle on King's Mountain, where the Americans defeated Ferguson. Describe what you heard.

2. Patriotic Songs: Read the words of the song "God of Our Fathers" and the story behind it on page 101. If you play music, learn to play it. Notice that this hymn was selected to celebrate the 100-year anniversary of the adoption of our Constitution. Try to learn the words of all the verses this school year.

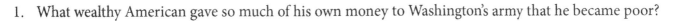

Questions

1. What wealthy American gave so much of his own money to Washington's army that he became poor?

2. What young officer traveled to France in 1779 to beg the French government for more help for the patriots?

3. What French officer was in charge of the French soldiers sent to America in answer to Lafayette's plea?

4. What officer went to Virginia to oppose the raiding force of Benedict Arnold?

5. Why did so much depend on the skill of the American generals and the spirit of their men?

6. Who was Dan Morgan's cavalry commander at Cowpens?

7. Who attacked Dan Morgan's force at Cowpens?

8. What action did Cornwallis take when he learned of Tarleton's defeat at Cowpens?

9. At what river did a providential circumstance slow down Cornwallis in his pursuit of Morgan?

10. What two American officers defeated a Tory force on its way to reinforce Cornwallis?

11. Why was the Battle of Guilford Court House an American success even though the British held the field?

12. What British officer did Greene face at Camden?

13. What happened at the fort at Ninety-six?

14. What two American leaders combined forces to conquer Fort Cornwallis?

15. What did the British do after the Battle of Eutaw Springs?

Projects for Chapter 24

1. Journal Entry: Pretend you were able to watch the arrival of French ships and soldiers. Write about what you saw and what you thought about France's decision to help. There is very little money to take care of the soldiers. What do you think of your cousin, who has been fighting this whole time, but has not been paid and has had to get by on very little food?

2. Make your own front page of a newspaper. Pick your favorite battle or the event in this chapter you think is the most important. Write a headline describing the event at the top of a sheet of paper. Draw a picture beneath or beside it to illustrate what happened, and write two or three sentences describing the event. With the rest of the sheet of paper, pick two or three more events and make headlines for them. For each event, write one or two sentences describing the event.

Questions

1. Was Arnold respected by his new comrades in the British army?

2. Why did Washington want so badly to capture and punish Arnold?

3. Whom did General Washington and Major Lee choose to pretend to defect to the enemy to trap Arnold?

4. Why was Champe discharged after failing in his mission?

5. What officer did Washington send to Virginia to oppose Arnold?

6. What French force did Washington send to Virginia in hopes of capturing Arnold?

7. How many French ships actually went to Virginia?

8. What British general brought 2,000 men to help Arnold?

9. What did Lafayette do for his troops with the money he raised?

10. Why did Clinton order Cornwallis to send some of his men to New York?

11. How did Cornwallis make Lafayette think that most of his army was across the river so he would **attack** the rear guard?

12. Why did Cornwallis not follow Wayne and Lafayette into the swamp?

13. What new order came from Clinton just as Cornwallis was about to ship his men to New York?

14. What place did Cornwallis choose to occupy?

15. What bad news did Cornwallis receive at about the time the French ships arrived?

Projects for Chapter 25

1. Journal Entry: Pretend you have heard of the British troops' negative reaction to Benedict Arnold. Even though Arnold was helping the British now, why do you think the British soldiers didn't like him? Pretend you have also heard of the young French Lafayette urging his soldiers to stop deserting. What do you think of him? Is he too young? Do you think he will be like the French commanders on the French ships, who keep retreating?

2. Coloring Picture: Color this picture of the flag as it looked when Betsy Ross sewed it. Notice the 13 stars. Why do you think it has 13 stars?

Questions

1. What was Washington's plan in early 1781 to beat the British?

2. What city did Washington and Rochambeau discuss attacking later in the year?

3. Why did Washington decide to march south instead?

4. What was the name of the young soldier who carried a fake message for Washington and was captured?

5. Who were the "cowboys"?

6. What was the mood of the soldiers when they found out they were going south to attack Cornwallis?

7. Before what government body did the army parade in Philadelphia?

8. Why did Washington leave his army for a few days?

9. How long did it take the army to march from outside New York to Yorktown, Virginia?

10. What did Clinton do in hopes of drawing Washington back to the northern states?

11. What two groups who fought for the British were most likely to commit acts of brutality upon the patriots?

12. Who was the colonial governor who sided with the patriot cause in the War of Independence?

13. What did Tory Major Bromfield do when Colonel Ledyard surrendered the fort?

14. What brutal act did the redcoats commit against a group of wounded patriot soldiers?

15. Did the attack on New London succeed in turning Washington's attention away from Cornwallis?

Project for Chapter 26

1. Journal Entry: Pretend you have heard some of your distant relatives died or lost their homes and businesses in New London when Benedict Arnold attacked. What do you think of that? Do you wish America would surrender, so the war would stop? Or do you want to fight the British even more? What do you think of Benedict Arnold now?

Questions

1. What French admiral was in charge of the fleet at Yorktown?

2. What did de Grasse want to do that might have allowed Cornwallis to escape by sea?

3. What British officer was occupying Gloucester Point with his troops?

4. Why did the patriots need to take the redoubts that the British had built outside their main defenses?

5. Why did Captain Ogden's men have unloaded muskets as they attacked?

6. How did Cornwallis first try to break out of Yorktown on October 16?

7. Why did Cornwallis' second attempt to evacuate Yorktown fail?

8. What American officer received the surrender document?

9. What did Lincoln do with Cornwallis's sword after it was presented to him in surrender?

10. What happened to Cornwallis immediately after the surrender?

11. Who was on the way to help Cornwallis but arrived too late?

12. As the army celebrated, what happened to soldiers who had been arrested?

13. What was given as souvenirs to General Rochambeau and Admiral de Grasse?

14. What relative of Washington's was dying of fever right after the battle of Yorktown?

15. Who was sent to Georgia to fight the British, Tories, and Indians?

Projects for Chapter 27

1. Journal Entry: What do you think of Cornwallis's surrender? What do you think of George Washington? Pretend you were staying in Philadelphia, visiting relatives, when you were awakened by the watchmen yelling out, "Cornwallis is taken!" What did you think when you heard that in the middle of the night? Were you surprised? What did you do? What did your relatives do?

2. Project: Make a poster, announcing the upcoming national day of thanksgiving and rejoicing at your church on December 13, commemorating Washington's victory over Cornwallis. What activities will there be? Will someone lead a prayer of thanksgiving? Who? Will there be a band or a choir to perform hymns of gratitude for God's deliverance? Will there be food?

Questions

1. Why did the Americans not have a navy at the beginning of the war?

2. How many prizes were believed to have been captured by American privateers?

3. What Scottish captain became an American naval hero?

4. Where was Jones ordered to concentrate his fighting?

5. What was the name of the French captain who served under Jones but was a great source of trouble for him?

6. What two British warships did Jones' squadron engage off the coast of Flamborough Head?

7. What were these ships doing in that region?

8. What was Jones' reply when called upon to surrender?

9. What did Jones do when the *Serapis* ran into his ship?

10. What happened to the *Bon Homme Richard* after the battle?

11. Where was the British fort attacked by American militia and ships in 1779?

12. Why was Lovell's battery not effective against the fort?

13. Why was the American ground attack broken off suddenly?

14. Was the French fleet very helpful in defending the coast of America?

15. How many of the American ships survived the expedition to Penobscot?

Project for Chapter 28

1. Journal Entry: Pretend you have heard about John Paul Jones' bloody victory against the British ship *Serapis*. Describe the battle. What do you think of Jones' courage? Write a comparison of the *Bon Homme Richard* and the *Serapis*.

Questions

1. Besides American independence, what important issue was settled by the fighting in the Ohio Country?

2. What mountain range stood west of the colonies?

3. What was the name of the region west of the Alleghenies and north of the Ohio River?

4. What fort was used by the British to organize and arm their Indian allies?

5. What was the nickname of the British officer, Henry Hamilton?

6. Why couldn't Forts Pitt, Randolph, and Henry defend the settlers against Indian attacks?

7. What American general led an unsuccessful raid on Mingo towns where the British had war supplies stored?

8. Who was the Tory who defected from General Hand's company and became a famous traitor?

9. What fort was built on the north side of the Ohio River but soon abandoned?

10. Why was the fort abandoned?

11. What American soldier was the top commander in the war west of the Alleghenies?

12. What fort did Clark capture after having marched his men through bitter cold weather and a flooded Wabash Valley?

13. Why did Jefferson not try "Hair-buyer" Hamilton for war crimes?

14. What important British fort did Rogers and Jefferson make plans to capture?

15. Why did their plan fail?

Project for Chapter 29

1. Journal Entry: Pretend you are one of George Rogers Clark's men who marched through the cold weather and flooded Wabash Valley. Describe how it felt. Tell why it was important enough for you to endure.

Questions

1. Why did Franklin reject the first British suggestions for arranging peace?

2. What two statesmen went to join Franklin in negotiating for peace with England?

3. How long did it take to work out a tentative agreement with England?

4. What treaty officially ended the war?

5. What document united the states before the Constitution was written?

6. What concern did the soldiers have as the time of their discharge drew near?

7. Did Congress have funds to pay the soldiers?

8. What did some angry soldiers do to force Congress to pay them?

9. To where did Congress move after meeting with the rebellious soldiers?

10. Why did Congress choose to move to Princeton?

11. On what day did the British march out of New York and the American army march in?

12. Who gave a dinner for the officers of the army at Fraunce's Tavern?

13. What event happened at Fraunce's Tavern on the next day?

14. Why did Washington meet with Congress on December 23, 1783?

15. How many times did Washington mention God, heaven, or providence in his brief speech?

Projects for Chapter 30

1. Journal Entry: Pretend you were able to witness George Washington resigning from the army. What did the hall look like? How did the crowd react to Washington's words? What did you think of Washington? Describe the cheering of the crowds when George Washington left.

2. Pretend you are one of George Washington's neighbors and you would like to visit him when he arrives home. Think of a gift you could bring to show him your appreciation for fighting for your freedom. What would your gift be? Why?

Questions

1. What did Noah Webster say was the source of republican principles of government?

2. How did Washington react when people suggested he should be made king?

3. What document governed the union of the states before the Constitution was written?

4. Who served as president of the Constitutional Convention?

5. Why was religious freedom protected in the Constitution?

6. How long did it take for all 13 states to ratify the Constitution?

7. Who was the first man to sign the Constitution?

8. What are the three branches of government under the Constitution?

9. Under the Constitution, who is the commander-in-chief of the armed forces?

10. What act of devotion did Washington do immediately after taking the oath of office?

11. What two things must our government provide in order for our country to work?

12. Who has the responsibility to receive foreign visitors to America?

13. Who makes federal laws for America?

14. Who has the power to declare war?

15. For how long are Supreme Court justices appointed?

Project for Chapter 31

1. Journal Entry: Pretend your cousin never received any pay for his time of fighting in the war because the weak union of the states could not raise money to pay soldiers. However, one of the many reasons your cousin wanted to fight in the war was because of the king's unfair taxes. What do you think of this? Pretend you have read newspaper articles about the newly proposed Constitution. What do you think of the new government it proposes?

Questions

1. What was the western boundary of the United States when Washington was president?

2. How long did it take to get from New York to Boston by stagecoach?

3. What was the fastest means of travel?

4. What was the name of the big wagons that hauled goods through Pennsylvania?

5. How often were most newspapers published?

6. What kind of eyeglasses were invented by Benjamin Franklin?

7. Where was the first library in America?

8. Where did the farmers get most of their food and clothing?

9. Were there many factories in the southern states?

10. Why was agriculture successful in the south?

11. Where was the United States capitol during most of Washington's presidency?

12. What was the name of the group who favored ratifying the Constitution?

13. Who served as Secretary of State in Washington's administration?

14. How did Britain violate the terms of the Treaty of Paris?

15. What is the name of the famous speech in which George Washington gave parting advice to America as he left the presidency?

Project for Chapter 32

1. Journal Entry: Pretend that George Washington has just put down the Whiskey Rebellion. What did you think of his decision? What do you think of the farmers who did not want to pay the tax? Do you think their resistance was justified? How do you think the whiskey tax was different from the taxes King George tried to levy?

Questions

1. Which signer was jokingly told that because of his light weight, he would kick longer than the other signers when he was hung by the British?

2. Which signer lost his job as justice of the peace because of his stand for independence?

3. How many of the signers of the Declaration served as soldiers during the War of Independence?

4. Which signer declined to go to England for cancer treatment so that he could work for independence in America?

5. Which signer, fleeing from the British, was actually helped to escape by men of the royal navy?

6. Which signer had two sons captured and imprisoned by the British?

7. Which signer was known as Honest John?

8. Which signer saw his wife imprisoned by the British for two years?

9. Which signer helped to melt a statue of King George and mold the lead into bullets?

10. Which signer issued a prayer proclamation and encouraged church attendance while governor of Pennsylvania?

11. Which signer started the Sunday school movement in America?

12. Which signer respected George Washington so much that he would not even joke about him?

13. Which signer was in prison when his home was burned and his wife died?

14. Which signer destroyed his own mansion with cannon fire?

Project for Chapter 33

1. Select one of the signers of the Declaration of Independence, and do additional research concerning the signer's birthplace, history, faith, and any other details you might find of interest, such as who was the youngest or oldest signer.

Questions

1. Which signer of the Constitution later served as governor of two different states?

2. Which signer signed the Constitution twice?

3. Which signer once scalded his arm so badly that he had to take a year off from his studies?

4. Which signer was the son of a Stamp Act tax collector?

5. Which signer loaned and gave away so much money that he went bankrupt at 64 years of age?

6. Which signer had helped to pay for Alexander Hamilton's education?

7. Which signer was arrested by the British for treason but released by a gang of patriot friends?

8. Who was the youngest signer at 26 years old?

9. Which signer had a brother hung in the Regulator movement?

10. Which signer would not take up arms against either England or America?

11. Which signer later served as secretary of war?

12. Which signer was governor of South Carolina in 1776 during the battle of Fort Moultrie?

13. Which signer joined the British army at age 11?

14. Which signer is known as the "Father of the Constitution"?

15. Which signers helped to get the Constitution ratified by writing the Federalist Papers?

Project for Chapter 34

1. Select one of the Amendments from the Constitution (such as Amendment I regarding Freedom of Religion, or Amendment II about the Right to Bear Arms) and do additional research on what that still means for us today.

History Quizzes

Questions: (20 Points Each Question)

1. What was the name of the great revival that swept the colonies before the War of Independence?

2. Did Congress approve Adams' suggestion to have George Washington lead the army?

3. How did Benedict Arnold get his first military experience?

4. Name three things forbidden by Washington's general orders of July 4, 1775.

5. Who made the first resolution urging a Declaration of Independence?

Questions: (20 Points Each Question)

1. Why did cannonballs do little damage to Fort Moultrie's walls?

2. Why did the British not see Washington's men being rowed to safety after the sun came up?

3. How did General Mifflin fool the British into believing that Washington's army was still in camp?

4. Who led the sharpshooters who did so much damage to Burgoyne's army?

5. What did John Adams say America must do to be able to hold her posts?

Questions: (20 Points Each Question)

1. What nation agreed to help America fight England?

2. Who is sometimes called the Father of the American Navy?

3. How long did Washington say that his men were sometimes without bread?

4. What wealthy American gave so much of his own money to Washington's army that he became **poor**?

5. Before what government body did the army parade in Philadelphia?

Questions: (20 Points Each Question)

1. What was John Paul Jones' reply when called upon to surrender?

2. What treaty officially ended the war?

3. What did Noah Webster say was the source of republican principles of government?

4. What are the three branches of American government under the Constitution?

5. Where was the United States capitol during most of Washington's presidency?

Questions: (20 Points Each Question)

1. I was one of the wealthiest men in the colony. I signed the Declaration of Independence with large handwriting so King George would be sure to see it. Who am I?

2. I said, "On the mercy of my Redeemer, I rely for salvation and on His merits; not on the works I have done in obedience to his precepts. " Who am I?

3. I rode 80 miles through a driving thunderstorm to cast my vote for independence. It was the deciding vote. Who am I?

4. My estate in New York was overrun by the British. I later served my country in the New York Senate as a representative in the first Congress. Who am I?

5. I became an invalid as a result of the harsh treatment I received in prison, where I was repeatedly beaten and kept near starvation. Who am I?

6. Who said, "I believe that there is only one living and true God, existing in three persons, the Father, the Son, and the Holy Ghost . . . and that at the end of the world, there will be a judgment of all mankind, when the righteous shall be publically acquitted before Christ the Judge, and be admitted to everlasting life and glory, and the wicked be sentenced to everlasting punishment."

7. I formed a band of patriots that used guerrilla-like tactics to harass Cornwallis on his drive northward. Who am I?

8. I considered it "a duty of every man to contribute, by every means within his power, to the welfare of his country, without expecting pecuniary rewards. Who am I?

9. I was captured and imprisoned after the British ravaged my South Carolina plantation. Who am I?

10. I was poisoned by a nephew who suspected I would leave my fortune to a slave whom I treated as a son. Who am I?

11. I was a good friend of John Paul Jones, whom I outfitted with a ship Jones used to harass the British navy. Who am I?

12. I sacrificed my fortune for the cause, financing a number of enterprises, including the Ticonderoga offensive. Who am I?

13. Even though my 150,000-acre estate was seized by the British, I continued to contribute my then dwindling fortune to Congress for the war effort. Who am I?

14. I was a church music director and set the entire Book of Psalms to music. Who am I?

15. I delivered a sentence to a man and then preached to him an exhortation to accept Jesus Christ as his Savior right away, before his death, so he could spend eternity in heaven rather than hell. Who am I?

16. My staunch support of the cause of the patriots led to my dismissal of the post of justice of the peace by the Royal Governor and to the burning of my house. Who am I?

17. I was forced to flee to the woods when hunted by the British. I lived for over a year in caves and hollows. I had to sleep with a dog one December night to stay warm. Who am I?

18. My Westchester, New York, estate was ransacked by the British, and nearly 1,000 acres were burned. My home was destroyed, my cattle butchered, and my family driven from home. Who am I?

●

19. I had such a love of justice; this principle was so deeply and indelibly impressed upon my heart, that in whatever situation of life I was placed, I was steadfastly and strenuously its advocate and promoter. Who am I?

20. I was present when the statue of King George was taken down at the reading of the Declaration of Independence in New York. I took the broken pieces of the headless statue home to Connecticut, where my wife, daughter, son, and neighbor ladies melted it down, making over 42,000 bullets that I later used to fight the British at the Battle of Saratoga. Who am I?

21. I was wounded and captured. After release, I served as governor and chief justice of Georgia and as a U.S. senator. Who am I?

● 22. My rice plantation was destroyed by the British, but my family escaped to the north. Who am I?

23. Once a British captain went out of his way to sail up the Cape Fear River to a point about 3 miles from Wilmington, where he shelled my house. Who am I?

24. I drafted a statewide prayer proclamation for my own state of Pennsylvania. I also recommended Christianity in the state's public schools and worked to raise church attendance in the state. Who am I?

25. I said, "My only hope of salvation is in the infinite, transcendent love of God manifested to the world by the death of His Son upon the Cross. Nothing but his blood will wash away by sins." Who am I?

● 26. I served in the army and was taken prisoner. The British raided my plantation while I was in prison and burned my buildings. My wife became ill and died before I was released. Who am I?

27. I sought a spot where I could witness the signature of each of the signers during the signing of the Declaration. Who am I?

28. I said, "I entreat you in the most earnest manner to believe in Jesus Christ, for there is salvation in no other." I was a minister of the gospel who trained other ministers. Who am I?

29. The British burned my home and seized my wife. She was held in a prison with no bed and no change of clothes and fed from a slop bucket. She was finally released after two years of suffering. Who am I?

30. I said, "I rely on the merits of Jesus Christ for a pardon for my sins." Who am I?

31. I wanted reconciliation with Great Britain at first, but came to realize, "It seems essential to our very existence as a free people, and without it we may soon be constrained to bid adieu to independence, to liberty, and safety — blessings, which from the justice of our cause, and favour of our Almighty Creator, visibly manifested in our protection, we have reason to expect, if in an humble dependence on his divine providence, we strenuously exert the means which are placed in our power." Who am I?

32. In attempting to move my family to escape the British, it turned out that they actually assisted my family without realizing who we were. Who am I?

33. It was later reported that my character as Christian, a father, a husband, and a friend was bright and unblemished. Who am I?

34. I said, "I have sworn upon the altar of God, eternal hostility against every form of tyranny over the mind of men." I also penned the Declaration of Independence. Who am I?

35. This was said of me, "Possessed of ample wealth, he used it like a philosopher and Christian in dispensing its blessing, for the benefit of his country and his fellow men." Who am I?

36. At the Battle of Yorktown, I turned one cannon on my own home and lit the fuse, killing two British officers inside. In so doing I destroyed all my earthly possessions. Who am I?

37. I contributed around one million dollars to finance the war effort. Who am I?

38. I was the second signer to die. I died in a duel. Who am I?

39. I had two sons in the Continental Army, both of whom received harsh treatment from the hand of the British. One only survived because a fellow prisoner pushed breadcrumbs to him through the key hole. Who am I?

40. I wanted to help fight as a soldier even though I was starting to suffer from a heart condition that caused me to faint at times. Who am I?

41. I lost more than 100 ships during the Revolution. Who am I?

42. I was criticized bitterly by many of my Pennsylvania neighbors for breaking the tie vote of the PA delegation in favor of independence. Who am I?

43. I loved to tell jokes, but there were two things I would not joke about. One was religion and the other was George Washington, whom I loved and admired. Who am I?

44. I was among the first captives and imprisoned at St Augustine, Florida, where "dangerous" rebels were held. Who am I?

45. My hand shook as I signed because of a recent stroke. I remarked that my signature was shaky, but not my resolve. Who am I?

46. The British sank nearly every merchant ship I owned. Who am I?

47. When the British raided their way through Virginia, I was head of the legislature and had to flee from town to town to keep from being captured. Who am I?

48. I declared: "I am constrained to express my adoration of . . . the Author of my existence, in full belief of . . . His forgiving mercy revealed to the world in Jesus Christ, for there is salvation in no other." Who am I?

49. I was a dynamic speaker with a powerful voice and was one of the first to declare that Britain had no authority to rule over the colonies. Who am I?

50. I began my life in America as a bondservant. Who am I?

51. By 1775 I believed that America must become independent. "The die is now cast. Sink or swim, live or die, survive or perish with my country is my unalterable determination." I told my wife Abigail, "We have appointed a continental fast. Millions will be upon their knees at once before the great Creator, imploring his forgiveness and blessing; He smiles on American councils and arms." Who am I?

52. I was such a slight, thin man that one of my fellow signers is said to have told me that if all the signers were hanged by the British I would be the unluckiest because I was so light that I would kick the longest. Who am I?

53. I rode 150 miles in two days to sign the Declaration of Independence. Who am I?

54. I poured thousands of dollars of my own personal fortune into clothing the American soldiers. Who am I?

Patriotic
Song Lyrics

My Country 'Tis of Thee (America)
by Samuel Smith

My country, 'tis of thee,
Sweet land of liberty,
Of thee I sing;
Land where my fathers died,
Land of the pilgrims' pride,
From every mountainside
Let freedom ring!

My native country, thee,
Land of the noble free,
Thy name I love;
I love thy rocks and rills,
Thy woods and templed hills;
My heart with rapture thrills,
Like that above.

Let music swell the breeze,
And ring from all the trees
Sweet freedom's song;
Let mortal tongues awake;
Let all that breathe partake;
Let rocks their silence break,
The sound prolong.

Our fathers' God to Thee,
Author of liberty,
To Thee we sing.
Long may our land be bright,
With freedom's holy light,
Protect us by Thy might,
Great God our King.

"My Country 'Tis of Thee" (also known as "America") is a patriotic hymn written by Samuel F. Smith in 1832, while a student at Andover Theological Seminary in Andover, Massachusetts. The melody had traveled around Europe in several variations, including "God Save the King." Even Beethoven and Haydn had used the music in some of their own compositions.

The song was the lyrical result of Samuel Smith's drive to create a national hymn for the United States. He wrote the now-classic anthem in about 30 minutes on a rainy day. The first three verses encourage and invoke national pride, while the last verse was specifically reserved as a petition to God for His continued favor and protection of the United States of America.

"My Country 'Tis of Thee" was first performed on July 4, 1832, at the Park Street Church in Boston, Massachusetts. Remarkably, about 500 Sunday school children premiered the piece at a memorable Independence Day celebration.

Samuel F. Smith was a Baptist minister, author, and journalist. He was born in Boston, Massachusetts, in 1801. He was later a student at Harvard and served as a translator for various foreign languages. He received his theological training at Andover Theological Seminary starting in 1830. He later married Mary White Smith and they had six children.

In addition to writing "My Country 'Tis of Thee," Smith wrote over 150 other hymns. These hymns were compiled into a Baptist hymnal, *The Psalmist*.

Smith died on November 16, 1895.

The Star Spangled Banner

by Francis Scott Key

Oh, say can you see by the dawn's early light

What so proudly we hailed at the twilight's last gleaming?

Whose broad stripes and bright stars thro' the perilous fight,

O'er the ramparts we watched were so gallantly streaming?

And the rocket's red glare, the bombs bursting in air,

Gave proof thro' the night that our flag was still there.

Oh, say does that star-spangled banner yet wave

O'er the land of the free and the home of the brave?

On the shore, dimly seen through the mists of the deep,

Where the foe's haughty host in dread silence reposes,

What is that which the breeze, o'er the towering steep,

As it fitfully blows, half conceals, half discloses?

Now it catches the gleam of the morning's first beam,

In full glory reflected now shines in the stream:

'Tis the star-spangled banner! Oh long may it wave

O'er the land of the free and the home of the brave!

And where is that band who so vauntingly swore

That the havoc of war and the battle's confusion,

A home and a country should leave us no more!

Their blood has washed out their foul footsteps' pollution.

No refuge could save the hireling and slave

From the terror of flight, or the gloom of the grave:

And the star-spangled banner in triumph doth wave

O'er the land of the free and the home of the brave!

Oh! thus be it ever, when freemen shall stand

Between their loved home and the war's desolation!

Blest with victory and peace, may the heav'n rescued land

Praise the Power that hath made and preserved us a nation.

Then conquer we must, when our cause it is just,

And this be our motto: "In God is our trust."

And the star-spangled banner in triumph shall wave

O'er the land of the free and the home of the brave.

It was 1814, and British General Ross and his soldiers were advancing on the city of Baltimore, determined to crush it as they had Washington, D.C. To support the ground attack, Admiral Sir George Cockburn began moving his ships upriver toward Baltimore on Sunday, September 12. The only barrier in his path was a small American outpost, Fort McHenry. The pentagon-shaped fort housed 57 guns and 1,000 soldiers under the command of Lieutenant Colonel George Armistead. It was Armistead who, a year earlier as a major, had commissioned the creation of the huge flag that flew from the center of Fort McHenry. On Monday morning the attack, which would ultimately last for 25 hours, began. Francis Scott Key and his two American friends, Dr. William Beanes and Colonel Skinner, were transferred to their sloop behind the convoy of British warships. They could only watch helplessly from its ramparts, closely guarded by the same enemy that was simultaneously killing their countrymen.

His sloop alone in the bay, Francis Scott Key looked fearfully toward the shoreline. A breeze began to move across the water's surface, and the smoke of battle began to shift ever so slightly to reveal patches of blue sky. And then, in the distant blue there appeared new colors . . . red and white . . . brief glimpses of the two-foot-wide stripes of the Star Spangled Banner. Then a star appeared in the daytime sky, then another . . . then 15 stars in the daytime. What a welcomed sight they were. Mr. Key's heart swelled with hope, and pride in the men who had so valiantly fought through the night to keep that flag flying. Reaching into his pocket, he withdrew an envelope and began to write his thoughts:

> O, say! can you see, by the dawn's early light,
>
> What so proudly we hail'd at the twilight's last gleaming?
>
> Whose broad stripes and bright stars, thro' the perilous fight,
>
> O'er the ramparts we watched were so gallantly streaming?
>
> And the rockets' red glare, the bombs bursting in air,
>
> Gave proof thro' the night that our flag was still there.
>
> O say! does that Star-Spangled Banner yet wave
>
> O'er the land of the free and the home of the brave?

As Mr. Key's sloop moved through the lifting curtain of battle smoke toward Baltimore, the 35-year-old attorney continued to work on his poem. Later in the day, in his room at Baltimore's Indian Queen Hotel, he cleaned up his copy on fresh paper, added a few more lines, and titled the four-stanza treatise "Defence of Fort M'Henry." His brother-in-law saw the poem and had a local printer make copies. Within days a polished-up version appeared in the *Baltimore American*, then in other newspapers and publications. He never knew that his poem, the "Star Spangled Banner," would become our national anthem. It was not officially recognized as such until 1931.

http://www.homeofheroes.com/hallofheroes/1st_floor/flag/1bfc_anthem.html, used by permission from Doug Sterner. Check out his site for valuable information.

America, The Beautiful

by Katharine Lee Bates – 1913

O beautiful for spacious skies,
For amber waves of grain,
For purple mountain majesties
Above the fruited plain!
America! America! God shed His grace on thee,
And crown thy good with brotherhood
From sea to shining sea!

O beautiful for pilgrim feet,
Whose stern impassion'd stress
A thoroughfare for freedom beat
Across the wilderness!
America! America! God mend thine ev'ry flaw,
Confirm thy soul in self-control,
Thy liberty in law!

O beautiful for heroes proved
In liberating strife,
Who more than self their country loved,
And mercy more than life!
America! America! May God thy gold refine
Till all success be nobleness,
And ev'ry gain divine!

O Beautiful for patriot dream
That sees beyond the years
Thine alabaster cities gleam,
Undimmed by human tears!
America! America! God shed His grace on thee,
And crown thy good with brotherhood
From sea to shining sea!

The author of "America the Beautiful," Katharine Lee Bates, was born in Falmouth, Massachusetts, in 1859 and grew up near the rolling sea. Her graceful poetic style came through in poems such as "The Falmouth Bell":

Never was there lovelier town
Than our Falmouth by the sea.
Tender curves of sky look down
On her grace of knoll and lea. . . .

Bates, who eventually became a full professor of English literature at Wellesley College, made a lecture trip to Colorado in 1893, and there she wrote the words to "America the Beautiful." As she told it, "We strangers celebrated the close of the session by a merry expedition to the top of Pike's Peak, making the ascent by the only method then available for people not vigorous enough to achieve the climb on foot nor adventurous enough for burro-riding. Prairie wagons, their tail-boards emblazoned with the traditional slogan, 'Pike's Peak or Bust,' were pulled by horses up to the half-way house, where the horses were relieved by mules. We were hoping for half an hour on the summit, but two of our party became so faint in the rarified air that we were bundled into the wagons again and started on our downward plunge so speedily that our sojourn on the peak remains in memory hardly more than one ecstatic gaze. It was then and there, as I was looking out over the sea-like expanse of fertile country spreading away so far under those ample skies, that the opening lines of the hymn floated into my mind."

On July 4, 1895, Bates' poem first appeared in *The Congregationalist*, a weekly newspaper. Bates revised her lyrics in 1904, a version published that year in *The Boston Evening Transcript*, and made some final additions to the poem in 1913. (For the story behind this patriotic song, see http://lcweb2.loc.gov/diglib/ihas/loc. natlib.ihas.200000001/default.html.)

God of Our Fathers

by George William Warren and Daniel C. Roberts

God of our fathers, whose almighty hand
Leads forth in beauty all the starry band
Of shining worlds in splendor through the skies
Our grateful songs before Thy throne arise.

Thy love divine hath led us in the past,
In this free land by Thee our lot is cast,
Be Thou our Ruler, Guardian, Guide and Stay,
Thy Word our law, Thy paths our chosen way.

From war's alarms, from deadly pestilence,
Be Thy strong arm our ever sure defense;
Thy true religion in our hearts increase,
Thy bounteous goodness nourish us in peace.

Refresh Thy people on their toilsome way,
Lead us from night to never ending day;
Fill all our lives with love and grace divine,
And glory, laud, and praise be ever Thine.

The hymn was written in 1876 for a celebration of the Centennial Fourth of July, and sung at Brandon, Vermont, to the tune called "Russian Hymn." When our General Convention appointed a Commission to revise the Hymnal, I sent it, without my name, promising to send the name if the hymn were accepted. It was accepted and printed anonymously in the report of the Commission. Before the Hymnal was printed, the Reverend Dr. Tucker, late of Troy, editor of our best musical Hymnal, and Mr. George William Warren, organist of St. Thomas' Church, New York, were appointed to choose a hymn for the centennial celebration of the adoption of the Constitution. They selected this hymn, then anonymous, and wanting a tune, Mr. Warren composed a tune to which it has since been set in the *Tucker Hymnal*.

Music: *National Hymn*, George W. Warren, 1888 (MIDI, score). Warren wrote the tune.

War of Independence

Timeline

Relevant Events prior to War of Independence:

1215   Magna Carta was established — English law had some of its basis in Magna Carta and power of king was weakened

1620   Coming of the Pilgrims to America

1638   Printing Press brought to America and books and newspapers begin to spread

1638   Establishment of Harvard University for the propagation of the gospel

1692   Establishment of William and Mary

1700   Establishment of Yale for training of ministers of the gospel

1746   College of New Jersey, now Princeton led by John Witherspoon who trained ministers of the gospel

1738   King George III takes the throne

1739–1740   The French and Indian War where Britain ran up debts

1765   Sam Adams organizes "Sons of Liberty" at Old South Meeting House

March 22, 1765   Stamp Act — Britain requires all legal documents to have a tax stamp affixed to them

March 24, 1765   Quartering Act — colonists are required to provide for the physical needs of British soldiers, permitting them to stay in their home and eat their food

March 18, 1766   Stamp Act repealed

June 29, 1767   Townshend Acts — tax on paper, lead, glass, and tea shipped from England

March 15, 1770   Boston Massacre — British troops fire on colonists

April 12, 1770   Parliament repeals Townshend Acts except tax on tea

November 2, 1772   Committees of Correspondence begun by Samuel Adams

May 10, 1773   Tea Act imposed, forcing colonists to buy tea from East India Company

December 16, 1773	Colonists disguised as Indians dump 342 chests of tea into Boston Harbor
1774	Coercive (Intolerable) Acts enforced by British to try to restore order to Massachusetts following Boston Tea Party
June 1, 1774	Boston Port Bill — British closed port of Boston to force colonists to pay for the tea
June 2, 1774	Reactivation of Quartering Act
September 5–October 26, 1774	Meeting of First Continental Congress — met at Carpenter's Hall
September-October, 1774	Groups of minutemen begin to form
December 22, 1774	Greenwich Tea Party
January 27, 1775	General Gage authorized to use force to maintain royal order in Massachusetts
February 21, 1775	Massachusetts Committee of Safety votes to purchase military equipment for 15,000 men
March 22, 1775	Edmund Burke makes speech in House of Commons to try to urge British government to reconcile with American colonies
April 19, 1775	Shots are fired at the Battle of Lexington; the Battle of Concord where weapons depot destroyed; "minutemen" force British troops back to Boston; George Washington takes command of the Continental Army and the Revolutionary War begins
April 23, 1775	The Provincial Congress in Massachusetts orders 13,600 American soldiers to be mobilized, and volunteers begin a year long Siege of Boston which is held by the British
May 5, 1775	Meeting of Second Continental Congress
June 17, 1775	Battle of Bunker Hill
June 17, 1775	Death of Dr. Joseph Warren
July 3, 1775	Washington takes command of the Continental Army
July 5, 1775	Olive Branch Petition aimed at reconciliation with Great Britain, which failed

July 6, 1775	Declaration on the Causes and Necessity of Taking Up Arms stating that Americans are "resolved to die free men rather than live as slaves"
December 31, 1775	The Battle of Quebec — British victory
January 1776	Thomas Paine's *Common Sense* published, providing strong arguments for American independence
January 24, 1776	Henry Knox arrives in Cambridge with guns and cannons from Fort Ticonderoga
February 27, 1776	Battle of Moore's Creek Bridge
March 5, 1776	Henry Knox arrives at Dorchester Heights with guns from Ticonderoga
March 4–17, 1776	Americans capture Dorchester Heights and British evacuate Boston (not knowing Americans don't have enough powder to fire the guns)
April 13, 1776	General Washington and main army arrive in New York
May 2, 1776	Americans gain support from King Louis XVI of France partly through Benjamin Franklin's efforts
June 6, 1775	General Howe and British fleet arrive off Sandy Hook, New Jersey
June 7, 1776	Richard Henry Lee submits his resolution to the Continental Congress for America to declare its independence from Britain
June 28, 1776	Battle of Sullivan's Island under command of Moultrie
July 1-7, 1776	British army of 32,000 arrives at Staten Island
July 1, 1776	Congress approves Richard Henry Lee's resolution
July 2, 1776	Congress votes for independence
July 4, 1776	Declaration of Independence is approved and signed by John Hancock
July 10, 1776	Declaration of Independence is read in New York and King George statue taken down
August 1, 1776	Sir Henry Clinton and his troops arrive at Staten Island from Charleston
August 2, 1776	Most of the signers of the Declaration of Independence affix their signatures to the document (a few are not present and do it later)

August 22, 1776	General Howe and his 15,000 troops arrive on Long Island
August 27–29, 1776	Battle of Long Island — British victory; General Sullivan is captured
August 29-30, 1776	General Washington and his 10,000 troops miraculously evacuate Long Island with the aid of a thick fog
September 16, 1776	Battle of Harlem Heights — the success does much to help restore American morale
September 21, 1776	British occupied New York breaks out in fire; one fourth of the city is burned
September 22, 1776	Nathan Hale is executed by the British, stating in his last words, "I regret that I have but one life to lose for my country"
October 11, 1776	Battle of Valcour Island
October 28, 1776	Battle of White Plains force General Washington to retreat to the west pursued by Cornwallis
November 16, 1776	Battle of Fort Washington — American garrison of 2,800 surrenders to British
November 21, 1776	General Washington begins retreat across New Jersey to the Delaware River
December 12, 1776	General Washington arrives at Trenton, New Jersey
December 12, 1776	Congress flees to Baltimore
December 26, 1776	General Washington and his men cross the Delaware River, attack and defeat Hessian garrison of 1,400
December 30, 1776	Washington gives speech urging his men to re-enlist
December 31, 1776	Benjamin Franklin arrives in Paris to negotiate for French aid to Americans
January 3, 1777	American victory at Battle of Princeton
January 6, 1777	Washington goes into winter quarters at Morristown, New Jersey
March 4, 1777	Congress adjourns at Baltimore, returns to Philadelphia

April 26, 1777	Sybil Luddington, daughter of Colonel Luddington, rides 40 miles on horseback to call militia to arms
April 26, 1777	British raid on Danbury, Connecticut, a force of 2,000 under General Tryon, destroy barns, homes, and storehouses
June 14, 1777	Congress ordains "Stars and Stripes" flag designed by Francis Hopkinson, signer of the Declaration, sewn by Betsy Ross, as Flag Day
July 6, 1777	Burgoyne recaptures Ft. Ticonderoga
July 27, 1777	Marquis de Layfayette arrives in Philadelphia
July 31, 1777	Congress commissions Layfayette as Major General
August 1, 1777	Washington and Layfayette meet for the first time and a lifelong friendship begins
August 16, 1777	American victory at Battle of Bennington
August 2–22, 1777	Battle of Fort Schuyler
September 11, 1777	The Battle of Brandywine — American defeat
September 19, 1777	Battle of Freemans Farm or Bemis Heights
October 4, 1777	Battle of Germantown — British victory
October 7, 1777	Battle of Saratoga — American victory — Morgan and his riflemen
October 17, 1777	Americans capture Burgoyne and his army of 5,700 at Saratoga (this persuades French to join Patriots)
November 2, 1777	John Paul Jones sails the *Ranger* from Portsmouth, NH
November 15, 1777	Evacuation of Ft. Mifflin
December 2, 1777	John Paul Jones reaches Nantes, France
December 11, 1777	Washington leaves White Marsh for Valley Forge
December 17, 1777	King Louis XVI agrees to help Americans

December 19, 1777   Washington and his men winter at Valley Forge (2,000 men will die there)

February 23, 1778   Wilhelm von Steuben arrives at Valley Forge to drill troops

April 22–23, 1778   John Paul Jones raid on Whitehaven, England

May 8, 1778   Howe's replacement, Henry Clinton, arrives from New York

June 17, 1778   King Louis XVI declares war on England

June 19, 1778   Evacuation of Valley Forge troops

June 28, 1778   Battle of Monmouth, Molly Pitcher fills her husband's position

July 2, 1778   Continental Congress reconvenes in Philadelphia

July 3, 1778   Wyoming Valley Massacre

1778   Nancy Strong hangs her petticoats on the line as an informant in the Culper Spy Ring

July 4, 1778   George Rogers Clark captures Kaskaskia

July 8, 1778   Washington sets up headquarters at Westpoint

July 8, 1778   Count d'Estaing's French fleet arrives in Delaware Bay

July 20, 1778   George Roger's Clark troops occupy Vincennes

September 14, 1778   Congress appoints Benjamin Franklin minister to France

December 17, 1778   Col. Henry "hair-buyer" Hamilton takes western outpost of Vincennes

December 29, 1778   Battle of Savannah

January 29, 1779   Battle of Augusta

February 23–25, 1779	Battle of Vincennes — George Rogers Clark and his men force surrender of Henry "hair-buyer" Hamilton, which gives Clark contrvol of Illinois territory
May 23, 1779	Benedict Arnold reveals Washington's plans to the enemy
June 20, 1779	Battle of Stono Ferry
July 15, 1779	Battle of Stony Point — Mad Anthony Wayne recaptures Stony Point in surprise night time raid
September 23, 1779	John Paul Jones aboard the *Bon Homme Richard* captures the *Serapis*
May 12, 1780	Battle of Charlestown — American defeat
May 29, 1780	Battle of Waxhaw Creek
June 7, 1780	Hannah Caldwell is shot by the British
June 23, 1780	Rev. James Caldwell gives hymnals for wadding for guns in Springfield, NJ
August 16, 1780	Battle of Camden
October 1780	Champe pretends to defect to British to help capture Arnold
October 2, 1780	Benedict Arnold turns traitor
October 7, 1780	Battle of King's Mountain — Ferguson and 1,100 men captured by frontiersmen
October 14, 1780	Washington chooses Greene to replace Gates
January 1, 1781	Battle of Cowpens — Dan Morgan and his riflemen annihilate Tarleton
March 15, 1781	Battle of Guilford Courthouse, NC — Cornwallis wins, but it's a costly victory, as he retreats to Yorktown
April 1, 1782	Joe Bettys is hanged

September 8, 1781	Battle of Eutaw Springs South Carolina — General Greene victory
September 1781	Attack on Ft. Griswold
September 28–October 6, 1781	Siege of Yorktown begins
October 19, 1781	Battle of Yorktown — Cornwallis and his 7,000 men surrender to Washington
November 10, 1782	1,000 Kentucky riflemen devastate British-backed Shawnee Indians
November 30, 1782	Preliminary Peace Treaty is signed in Paris by British and Americans
December 14, 1782	British evacuate Charleston
January 20, 1783	Britain signs Peace Agreement with America and France
September 3, 1783	U.S. and Great Britain sign Peace Treaty in Paris and war is officially over
November 25, 1783	British evacuate New York City, their last holding in America
December 23, 1783	George Washington resigns his commission before Congress with tears, "commending the interests of our dear country to the protection of Almighty God"
May 25, 1787	Meeting of the Constitutional Convention to discuss writing a governing document to replace the Articles of Confederation
September 13, 1788	The Constitution of the United States of America is ratified and became the Supreme law of the land; the Unites States is born
April 30, 1789	George Washington, standing on the balcony of Federal Hall on Wall Street in New York, took his oath of office as the first President of the United States
April 30, 1789	George Washington's Inaugural Address

Answer Keys

America's Struggle to Become a Nation ➡ Worksheet Answer Keys

Chapter 1

Why a War of Independence?

1. Englishmen
2. Yes
3. The Great Awakening
4. Members of the Church of England who did not want to leave the church but wanted to see biblical reforms
5. It teaches us that we are all sinners who need a Savior
6. Yes
7. The colonists were being taxed by Parliament, but could not vote on their own representatives in Parliament.
8. They had just fought the French and Indian War with France.
9. 25,000
10. No
11. The colonies could only trade with England, not other countries.
12. No
13. Making finished products out of iron
14. They were extremely unpopular.
15. To enforce the Stamp Act and other unpopular laws

Chapter 2

Trouble Over Taxes

1. No
2. Patrick Henry
3. There was much public anger against them.
4. The colonists would not buy their products with the stamps on them.
5. Less than 1 year
6. Tories (or Loyalists)
7. They believed he was trying to establish his right to tax the colonies.
8. They believed he had not paid fees on goods the ship had delivered.
9. John Adams
10. The *Gaspee*

11. He thought their objection was to the price of tea (the objection was really to being taxed without representation in Parliament).
12. They sent the tea back to England.
13. They blackened their faces and dressed as Mohawk Indians.
14. No. No one was harmed, and the "Indians" even swept the decks before leaving.
15. Over one million dollars in today's money

Chapter 3

The First Battles

1. It prohibited ships from entering or leaving Boston Harbor.
2. The colonists could no longer elect their own leaders. The colony would be ruled by men appointed by the king.
3. It was an act that made all the territory east of the Mississippi River and north of the Ohio River part of Canada instead of the American colonies.
4. Georgia's colonial governor successfully prevented them from appointing delegates.
5. Benjamin Franklin
6. He wanted to keep the peace with the colonies.
7. General Howe's brother, Admiral Richard Howe
8. Patriot men who were prepared to leave their homes to fight at a minute's notice
9. No
10. To seize war materials stored there by the patriots
11. William Dawes
12. To give a better chance that at least one of them would get past British outposts and reach Concord
13. John Hancock and Samuel Adams
14. The patriots had been warned of their coming and had moved the supplies
15. Many of them had fought Indians and the French

Chapter 4

The Choice of a Leader

1. Men from other colonies hurried to Massachusetts to help.

2. Fort Ticonderoga fell and the Second Continental Congress met

3. John Hancock

4. He suggested that they be adopted as an official Continental Army and for Congress to raise money to support the army.

5. He thought the New England colonies would act without the other colonies to adopt and support the army.

6. He thought it would unite the colonies to have a southern commander over a mostly northern force.

7. Artemas Ward

8. Yes

9. No

10. Yes. They voted unanimously for Washington as commander of the army.

11. No

12. Nothing

13. Patsy

14. He joined the soldiers at Cambridge, outside Boston

Chapter 5

Arnold and Allen

1. He laid siege to the fort and starved the French out instead of making a frontal assault as Abercrombie had done.

2. Lake Champlain

3. Captain Delaplace

4. To get military supplies and open the way for an invasion of Canada

5. A farmer's son named Nathan Beman

6. In the name of the Great Jehovah and the Continental Congress

7. Crown Point

8. He tried to take command of the fort.

9. St. Johns

10. Return them to the British

11. His father turned to drink.

12. His family could no longer pay for his education.

13. He was apprenticed to cousins in the business.

14. Fighting in the French and Indian War

Chapter 6

The Battle of Bunker Hill

1. Yes

2. They used it to equip the militia.

3. Create their own government as a republic

4. It promised to forgive any patriot who would lay down his arms and swear loyalty to King George.

5. No. (Instead they decided to take action by fortifying a hill near Boston.)

6. Colonel Prescott

7. Reverend Samuel Langdon, president of Harvard College, offered a prayer for the men.

8. Breed's Hill had a better view of the town and the harbor where the British ships were.

9. Yes

10. It offered a better command of both the harbor and the town.

11. 3,000

12. No

13. They turned and fled down the hill

14. They were out of gunpowder

Chapter 7

Life in the New Army

1. Governor Tryon

2. He heard about the patriots' courage at Bunker Hill.

3. Organizing the army

4. Profane cursing, swearing, drunkenness

5. Attendance at divine services (worship meetings)

6. He organized them by colonies.

7. In the morning, after prayers

8. Massachusetts

9. A chaplain in Washington's army

10. No

11. Daniel Morgan's riflemen

12. Liberty or Death

13. The Fighting Quaker

14. Israel Putnam

15. Charles Lee

Chapter 8

Defeat and Victory in Battle

1. He did not like being lower in position than Ethan Allen.
2. Yes
3. Allen and Arnold
4. Schuyler fell sick and could not return to the campaign.
5. Fort Chambly and Fort St. John's
6. During the French and Indian War, with General Wolfe
7. Thirty-three days
8. The British simply stayed inside their fort.
9. Dan Morgan
10. Smallpox
11. Three hundred miles
12. Because cannons located there could bombard Boston and the Harbor
13. To distract the British from his move to the heights on the third night
14. He said that the patriots had done more work in one night than his men could have done in a month.
15. So that the British would not burn the town

Chapter 9

A Desire for Independence!

1. It was a last-ditch attempt to avoid war
2. No
3. The Proclamation of Rebellion
4. Set it on fire
5. He hired foreign mercenaries called Hessians.
6. North Carolina
7. Richard Henry Lee of Virginia
8. John Adams
9. He had left Congress for a time to care for his sick wife.
10. John Hancock and Charles Thompson
11. He expected the British to attack New York.
12. It was melted into bullets for the patriot army.
13. Oliver Wolcott

Chapter 10

Battles North and South

1. A group of people organized under a government
2. Their own representatives in their state governments
3. Their success in early battles such as Lexington & Concord, Bunker Hill, and the evacuation of Boston
4. General Henry Clinton
5. To stop them from moving east to join forces with Clinton
6. Men from inland North Carolina who resisted the colonial government
7. Because some government officials were corrupt
8. Tryon built himself an extravagant mansion with taxpayers' money.
9. The North Carolina colonial militia
10. A North Carolina government official who was attacked by the Regulators for corruption
11. Charleston, South Carolina
12. Colonel William Moultrie
13. The cannonballs sank into the log-and-sand walls without breaking them down
14. General Charles Lee
15. The water was much deeper than Clinton had expected.

Chapter 11

A Miraculous Escape Questions

1. Halifax
2. There was strong Tory support in the area and much patriot wealth to be captured and used.
3. Make peace
4. On board a British ship
5. 500
6. Strengthening his defenses
7. Nathanael Greene
8. Greene got sick and had to leave.
9. There was a threat of Howe attacking New York City.
10. They sank old, rotten ships in the water.
11. General Howe

12. It was between two British armies.

13. The ocean tide was rising, making the creek deeper.

14. A contrary wind sprang up and slowed their progress.

15. A thick fog settled over the American position just as the sun came up.

Chapter 12

Battles Around New York

1. It was decided to evacuate the island and move the army to New York.

2. He built many campfires, as if many men were present.

3. No

4. An unexpected fog moved in suddenly.

5. The American General Sullivan, who had been captured in battle on Long Island

6. A primitive submarine

7. The *Eagle*, Admiral Howe's flagship

8. Ezra Lee, the *Turtle*'s pilot, could not screw his torpedo to the ship's hull because it struck metal plating.

9. He managed to blow up a barge with a floating bomb.

10. Captain Nathan Hale

11. Yes

12. No

13. Mistress Murray

14. The city caught on fire and most of it burned down.

15. By breathing through a goose quill

Chapter 13

Retreat and Victory

1. Colonel Magaw

2. 150

3. Nathanael Greene

4. Military supplies and cannon

5. He published another offer of pardon.

6. General Lee

7. Sail for home

8. The fishermen of General John Glover

9. The road was icy and a severe winter storm was upon the army.

10. Around 1,000

11. The horrible condition of the roads in winter.

12. He left fires burning and men digging for Cornwallis to hear.

13. Around 500

14. Thawing roads

15. No. Washington's army had already moved on.

Chapter 14

The Battle of Valcour Island

1. Trenton and Princeton

2. They wanted to divide the colonies into two parts.

3. Arnold and his men built the ships.

4. Five hours

5. The *Washington*

6. General Waterbury

7. Bettys turned traitor and was later hung for spying.

8. He was pardoned by the mercy of George Washington.

9. He had not taken the deerskin cover off the lock.

10. A tiny lead box with a coded message inside.

11. Ticonderoga

12. Winter was coming and he was afraid of getting his ships stuck in the ice on the lake.

13. No

14. Congress said that Connecticut already had enough generals.

15. Washington pleaded with Arnold to stay in the army.

Chapter 15

Burgoyne's Campaign Begins

1. "Britons never retreat."

2. Colonel Barry St. Leger

3. To seize war materials stored there

4. Set fire to the town

5. Benedict Arnold

6. Gentleman Johnny

7. 10,000

8. 3,000

9. A house in the fort caught fire and illuminated the scene.

10. Colonel Warner and Colonel Francis

11. The Hessians arrived to reinforce the British.

12. Fort Edward

13. Shoot some of the generals

14. Destroyed bridges and built obstacles in the roads

15. Colonel Baum

Chapter 16

Bennington and Fort Schuyler

1. Return to New Hampshire and recruit more soldiers

2. He felt that less qualified officers had been promoted over him.

3. They complained that they had been called out several times yet never allowed to fight.

4. He promised them that, once the sunshine came back, if he did not give them fighting enough, he would never call them out again.

5. The militiamen were wearing civilian clothing.

6. They were untrained and poorly armed and faced experienced troops.

7. The men from Manchester under Colonel Warner

8. He wondered about his Tory allies, supplies for his army, and the Indian forces leaving him.

9. Skiffs, bateaux, and canoes

10. Be strong and of a good courage; be not afraid

11. Hanyost Schuyler

12. Fake an escape and fool the British and Indians about the size of Arnold's force

13. He held his brother and threatened to hang him if Hanyost failed

14. Holes in his hat

15. It was the idea of Major Brooks

Chapter 17

The Downfall of Burgoyne

1. Daniel Morgan

2. Arnold and Gates

3. Colonel Kosciuszko

4. Benedict Arnold

5. Gates himself

6. Sir Henry Clinton

7. The left leg

8. Mrs. Schuyler

9. He inserted it into a small bullet.

10. It might have prolonged the fighting long enough for Clinton to arrive and help Burgoyne.

11. A plot to overthrow Washington and replace him with General Gates

12. At the home of General Schuyler near Albany

13. A very kind one

14. As intimate friends

15. It greatly increased the number of volunteers.

Chapter 18

Trying to Fool a Fox

1. Philadelphia

2. General Clinton

3. He had them move in different directions around New York so that Washington could not be sure where they were going.

4. He could not have gotten his army to Charleston before Howe.

5. 1,000

6. These actions kept Howe from being able to send help to Burgoyne.

7. He was informed by Tories.

8. He was known for having his men remove the flints from their muskets so they would have to fight with bayonets.

9. Fort Mercer and Fort Mifflin

10. Germantown

11. No

12. Valley Forge

13. Baron von Steuben

14. Mary Knight

15. Mary concealed him in a cider barrel in her cellar.

Chapter 19

A Turning Point in the War

1. France

2. Benjamin Franklin

3. She offered to grant all the demands the colonists had made early in the war.

4. Admiral d'Estaing

5. Burgoyne

6. They feared that New York would be the next city to be attacked now that the French had entered the war.

7. They feared the revenge of the patriot army in Valley Forge, now that the British would not be in the city to protect them.

8. He put them aboard ships intended for moving his army.

9. Only two were hung; the rest were eventually pardoned.

10. They returned to Philadelphia.

11. Send a fast detachment ahead of the army to engage Clinton until the rest of the army could come up

12. At Monmouth Court House

13. Very hot

14. One year

15. Mary Hayes, who took her husband's place serving a cannon when he went down in battle.

Chapter 20

Battles in Various Places

1. He hoped to keep Clinton confined in New York and keep the war dragging on until the British grew so tired of it that they gave up.

2. It was feared that the channels around the city were too shallow for the larger French ships.

3. Clinton sent 5,000 of his men from New York to assist British forces in the West Indies.

4. Former Tory neighbors and their Indian allies

5. General Sullivan

6. Mad Anthony Wayne

7. The Hudson

8. Wayne wanted to surprise the British soldiers in the fort and so attacked with bayonets.

9. Carry him into the fort so he could die at the head of his men

10. Kindly

11. John Paul Jones

12. Men who sailed privately owned ships in attacking British shipping

13. A Letter of Marque

14. Captain Adam Hyler

15. He spared one ship because a woman and some children were on board.

Chapter 21

The Fighting Preacher and Treason

1. General "Light Horse Harry" Lee, the father of Robert E. Lee

2. A gold medal

3. Reverend James Caldwell, who was known by the British as the "rebel high priest"

4. Pistols

5. They murdered his wife

6. The fall of Charleston, South Carolina

7. They distributed counterfeit money so that people did not want to accept continental money for payment.

8. He had gone deeply in debt through his lavish lifestyle while in Philadelphia.

9. West Point

10. Major John Andre

11. Eating breakfast with friends

12. He rode his horse to the river and was rowed to a British ship.

13. The *Vulture*

14. Order him to be shot instead of hanged

15. She was ordered to leave town.

Chapter 22

Suffering Soldiers

1. Both sides were content to hold the territory they controlled presently.

2. No

3. Five or six days

4. His soldiers foraging and stealing food from the farms

5. Mrs. Henry Knox and Mrs. Nathanael Greene

6. The Pennsylvania line under Mad Anthony Wayne

7. General Clinton sent messengers offering pardon and back pay to the Americans if they would agree to stop fighting.

8. Many who had volunteered for three-year enlistments had not been released at the end of that time.

9. March on Congress and present their claims to them

10. Provided them with rations to the best of his ability

11. To set him free on his promise not to fight again

12. With kindness, just as if they were their own soldiers

13. The king had declared all rebels to be traitors rather than prisoners of war.

14. Prison ships

15. Defect to the British

Chapter 23

The War in the South

1. Because they had not succeeded in conquering the Americans in the north and middle colonies

2. They hoped to be able to keep their southern colonies.

3. Midway

4. General Robert Howe

5. A local slave

6. General Benjamin Lincoln

7. General William Moultrie

8. About 450

9. The arrival of Count d'Estaing and the French fleet

10. Count Pulaski

11. British General Clinton and American General Lincoln

12. "Tarleton's quarter" referred to killing conquered enemies after they had surrendered.

13. The Americans under General Gates

14. Too many of his men were sick

15. The Battle of King's Mountain

Chapter 24

General Greene in the South

1. Robert Morris

2. Lafayette

3. Count Rochambeau

4. Baron von Steuben

5. Because the Americans were badly outnumbered by the British

6. Colonel William Washington, George Washington's cousin

7. The detachment of Banastre Tarleton

8. He went in pursuit of Morgan.

9. The Catawba River

10. Andrew Pickens and "Light Horse Harry" Lee

11. Because British losses were so high that they seriously damaged Cornwallis's army

12. Lord Rawdon

13. Greene besieged the fort but had to retreat when Lord Rawdon approached with reinforcements for the British.

14. Pickens and Lee

15. They returned to Charleston.

Chapter 25

Cornwallis Is Trapped

1. No

2. As an example to others who might consider becoming traitors

3. Sergeant-major John Champe

4. Because if captured he could have been hung as a deserter by the British

5. Lafayette

6. The entire French fleet and Rochambeau's army

7. Three

8. General Phillips

9. He bought them clothing.

10. Washington had fooled Clinton into thinking he was about to be attacked.

11. He spent three days moving baggage and equipment across, making it seem that most of his men were across also.

12. His superior numbers would not have helped him because it is hard to move large numbers of men in a swamp.

13. He was ordered to keep his men in Virginia and wait to be reinforced by British ships.

14. Yorktown

15. He learned that the combined French and American forces from the north were marching to attack him.

Chapter 26

Washington Marches South

1. He planned to wear them out with waiting rather than attacking in open battle.
2. New York
3. He received information that Cornwallis had bottled himself up in Yorktown.
4. Montagnie
5. Loyalist outlaws
6. They were delighted.
7. Congress
8. To visit his home, Mount Vernon
9. Three months
10. He ordered Benedict Arnold to attack New London, Connecticut.
11. The Tories and Hessians
12. Jonathan Trumbull of Connecticut
13. He murdered Ledyard with his own sword.
14. Put them in a cart and rolled them downhill into the river
15. No

Chapter 27

Cornwallis Surrenders

1. Count de Grasse
2. He wanted to leave Yorktown and fight newly arrived British ships in the area.
3. Col. Tarleton
4. Because from those positions they could easily fire at the Americans in their trenches.
5. So they could approach quietly and use their bayonets
6. He ordered Colonel Abercrombie to attack a part of the French line and break through.
7. A sudden storm scattered the boats in which his men were escaping.
8. General Benjamin Lincoln. The terms were the same he had received from Cornwallis when Lincoln had been forced to surrender Charleston to him the previous year.
9. Lincoln gave the sword back to the officer who presented it to him.
10. He was paroled and permitted to return to New York.

11. General Clinton and his troops
12. They were released.
13. Two captured cannon from Yorktown
14. His stepson, John Parke Custis
15. Mad Anthony Wayne

Chapter 28

A Strange War on the Sea

1. They had been British colonies before the war, and so had been defended by the British navy.
2. Around 700
3. John Paul Jones
4. Along the shores of Great Britain
5. Landais
6. The *Serapis* and the *Countess of Scarborough*
7. Protecting some merchant ships
8. "I have not yet begun to fight!"
9. He tied the two ships together.
10. The *Richard* sank the next day.
11. Penobscot, Maine
12. It was too far away.
13. A British rescue expedition arrived.
14. No
15. None of them

Chapter 29

War in the West

1. The issue of how much land belonged to America
2. The Allegheny Mountains
3. The Ohio Country
4. Fort Detroit
5. "Hair-buyer Hamilton"
6. Because the Indian war parties simply slipped between the forts
7. General Edward Hand
8. Simon Girty
9. Fort Laurens
10. Because the Americans did not have enough soldiers to protect the fort
11. George Rogers Clark
12. Fort Vincennes

13. Because the British threatened to treat American officers the same way.

14. Fort Detroit

15. Rogers could not get enough men to successfully attack Detroit.

Chapter 30

An Unsettled Peace

1. They did not allow for the independence of America.

2. John Adams and John Jay

3. Two months

4. The Treaty of Paris, 1783

5. The Articles of Confederation

6. They were concerned that they might be sent home without being paid for their service in the army.

7. No

8. They marched on Congress and met with the leaders.

9. They moved to Princeton, New Jersey.

10. The governor of New Jersey offered to protect them.

11. November 25, 1783

12. New York's Governor Clinton

13. Washington said farewell to his officers

14. To resign his commission

15. Three times

Chapter 31

The U.S. Constitution

1. The Bible and the Christian religion

2. He was offended by the suggestion.

3. The Articles of Confederation

4. George Washington

5. Because the Pilgrim Fathers had been persecuted in England for worshiping as they believed the Bible taught them to worship

6. One year

7. George Washington

8. Legislative, executive, judicial

9. The president

10. He kissed the Bible on which he had sworn.

11. Justice and protection

12. The president

13. The Congress

14. Congress

15. For life, as long as good behavior continues

Chapter 32

The New Republic

1. The Mississippi River

2. Six days

3. Horseback

4. Conestoga wagons

5. Weekly

6. Bifocals

7. Philadelphia

8. They produced it on their own farms.

9. No

10. Fertile soil and a long growing season

11. In Philadelphia

12. The Federalists

13. Thomas Jefferson

14. They refused to leave their forts in the west.

15. Washington's Farewell Address

Chapter 33

Who Were the Signers of the Declaration of Independence?

1. Elbridge Gerry

2. Josiah Bartlett

3. 16

4. Caesar Rodney

5. George Read

6. Abraham Clark

7. John Hart

8. Francis Lewis

9. Oliver Wolcott

10. Benjamin Franklin

11. Benjamin Rush

12. James Smith

13. Thomas Heyward Jr.

14. Thomas Nelson Jr.

Chapter 34

Who Were the Signers of the Constitution?

1. John Dickinson
2. George Read (once for himself and once for ailing colleague John Dickinson)
3. Gouvernor Morris
4. Jared Ingersoll
5. Thomas Fitzsimmons
6. William Livingstone
7. David Brearly
8. Jonathan Dayton
9. William Few
10. William Samuel Johnson
11. James McHenry
12. John Rutledge
13. Pierce Butler
14. James Madison
15. James Madison, Alexander Hamilton, and John Jay

America's Struggle to Become a Nation ◖ Quiz Answer Keys

First Semester–First Quarter

1. The Great Awakening
2. Yes, they voted unanimously
3. Fighting in the French and Indian War
4. Profane cursing, swearing, and drunkenness
5. Richard Henry Lee of Virginia

First Semester–Second Quarter

1. The cannonballs sank into the log and sand walls
2. A thick fog settled over the American position just as the sun came up
3. He built many campfires, as if many men were present
4. Daniel Morgan
5. Shoot some of the generals

Second Semester–Third Quarter

1. France
2. John Paul Jones
3. Five or six days
4. Robert Morris
5. Congress

Second Semester–Fourth Quarter

1. "I have not yet begun to fight!"
2. The Treaty of Paris, 1783
3. The Bible and the Christian religion
4. Legislative, executive, and judicial
5. Philadelphia

Bonus Quiz

Who Am I?

1. John Hancock
2. Charles Carroll
3. Caesar Rodney
4. William Floyd
5. Richard Stockton
6. Roger Sherman
7. John Penn
8. George Ross
9. Arthur Middleton
10. George Wythe
11. Joseph Hewes
12. William Williams
13. Lewis Morris
14. Francis Hopkinson
15. Thomas McKean
16. Josiah Bartlett
17. John Hart
18. Lewis Morris
19. Samuel Huntington
20. Oliver Wolcott
21. George Walton
22. Lyman Hall
23. William Hooper
24. Benjamin Franklin
25. Benjamin Rush
26. Thomas Heyward Jr.
27. William Ellery
28. John Witherspoon
29. Francis Lewis
30. Samuel Adams
31. Thomas Stone
32. George Read
33. Matthew Thornton
34. Thomas Jefferson
35. Francis Lightfoot Lee
36. Thomas Nelson
37. Robert Morris
38. Button Gwinnett
39. Abraham Clark
40. William Whipple
41. George Clymer
42. John Morton
43. James Smith
44. Edward Rutledge
45. Stephen Hopkinson
46. Carter Braxton

47. Benjamin Harrison
48. Robert Treat Paine
49. James Wilson
50. George Taylor
51. John Adams
52. Elbridge Gerry
53. Samuel Chase
54. William Paca

BIBLIOGRAPHY

Amstel, Marsha. *Sybil Ludington's Midnight Ride.* Minneapolis, MN: Millbrook Press, 2000.

Barton, David. *Original Intent.* Aledo, TX: Wallbuilders Press, 1996.

Blaisdell, Albert F., and Francis K. Ball. *Hero Stories from American History.* Boston, MA: Ball, Ginn and Co, 1903.

Boyer, Marilyn. *For You They Signed.* Green Forest, AR: Master Books, 2010.

Boyer, Marilyn, and Grace Tumas. *Portraits of Integrity.* Rustburg, VA: Learning Parent, 2012.

Boyer, Marilyn, and Grace Tumas. *Profiles of Valor: Character Studies from the War of Independence.* Rustburg, VA: Learning Parent, 2013.

Brooks, Elbridge S. *The Story of the United States.* Boston, MA: D. Lothrop and Co., 1891.

Brooks, Elbridge S. *The True Story of the United States of America: Told for Young People.* Boston, MA: Lothrop Publishing Co., 1891.

Eggleston, Edward. *A History of Our United States and Its People.* New York: American Book Co., 1888.

Federer, William. *American Minute: Notable Events of American Significance Remembered on the Date they Occurred.* St. Louis, MO: Amerisearch, Inc., 2003.

Fradin, Dennis Brindell. The Founders: *The 39 Stories Behind the U.S. Constitution.* New York: Walker and Co., 2005.

Kirkpatrick, Katherine. *Redcoats and Petticoats.* New York: Holiday House, 1999.

Mace, William H. *Mace's Beginner's History.* Chicago, IL: Rand McNally and Co., 1909.

Mace, William H. *Mace's Primary History: Stories of Heroism.* Chicago, IL: Rand MCNally and Co., 1909.

Mace, William H. *Mace's School History of the United States.* Chicago, IL: Rand, McNalley and Co., 1904.

Montgomery, D.H. *The Beginners American History.* Boston, MA: Ginn and Co., 1892.

Montgomery, D.H. *The Leading Facts of American History.* New York: Chautauqua Press, 1892.

Moore, Frank, and C.T. Evans. *Patriot Preachers of the American Revolution.* New York: Charles T. Evans, 1862.

Stevenson, Burton Egbert. *Poems of American History.* Boston and New York: Houghton Mifflin and Co., 1908.

Tomlinson, E.T. *Young Folks History of the Revolution.* New York: Grosset and Dunlap, 1901.

Wallbuilders.com resources.

White, Henry Alexander. *Beginners History of the United States: Stories of the Men Who Made Our Country.* New York: American Book Company, 1906.

RECOMMENDED RESOURCES

The following resources are suggested for further study.

AUDIOBOOKS

The following audios are all available as downloads through the **Uncle Rick Audio Club** (UncleRickAudios.com) or as CDs from **CharacterConcepts.com.**

Uncle Rick Reads America First by Lawton B. Evans. This audio is chock full of exciting stories from America's history, including stories about Paul Revere, King George and the Colonies, Ethan Allan and the Green Mountain Boys, Nathan Hale, Elizabeth Zane, Molly Pitcher, the Swamp Fox, Mad Anthony and the Capture of Stony Point, Ben Franklin, Nolichucky Jack, How Gen. Schuyler Was Saved, How Layfayette Came to America, Nancy Hart, Capturing the Hessians, and lots more!

Uncle Rick Reads American Fights and Fighters by Cyrus Townsend Brady. This book was written in 1900 to stimulate patriotism and love of country in young people. It covers some of the major battles fought in the War of Independence and War of 1812. Many of Dan Morgan's experiences are told.

Uncle Rick Reads Boys of Liberty Library Collection 1. In this collection of five great novels for young people, the early days of the War of Independence come vividly to life. Follow Paul Revere as he steals through dark streets of Boston, collecting and communicating information about the British, then galloping through the Middlesex farms and villages, calling the patriots to wake up and prepare for battle! Share the tense days and weeks of the siege of Boston. March with Ethan Allen and his Green Mountain Boys through some of the roughest conflicts of the early war. Thrill again to the peril and excitement of the Battle of Long Island! Collection includes: Paul Revere and the Boys of Liberty, Fooling the Enemy — A Story of the Siege of Boston, The First Shot for Liberty or the Minutemen of Massachusetts, Into the Jaws of Death or the Battle of Long Island, and The Hero of Ticonderoga or Ethan Allen and His Green Mountain Boys.

Uncle Rick Reads Boys of Liberty Collection 3. Step back in time as you experience the War of 1812 with excitement! Adventure! Heroes! The White House has been burned! Fort McHenry is under attack! Such were the agitated reports that echoed through the streets during the War of 1812. In this new set of Uncle Rick audio books, America's second war against British tyranny comes boldly to life! Thrill to the exciting stories of great sea battles in which mighty ships trade broadsides and boarding parties. Stand firm with Stephen Decatur and David Farragut as they fight the largest navy on earth with their infant navy — tiny, but full of courage and daring. Once again a dynamic chapter in the history of America is brought to life by Uncle Rick! Approx. 11 hours listening time. Appropriate for ages 8 through adult. (Boys of Liberty Collection)

Uncle Rick Reads Following Mad Anthony or the Drums of Germantown by T.C. Harbaugh. Uncle Rick reads this great account of Mad Anthony Wayne and the Battle of Germantown. You'll feel like you were there!

Uncle Rick Reads For Freedoms Cause or On to Saratoga. Learn all about the Battle of Saratoga told in a captivating story fashion.

Uncle Rick Reads Four American Pioneers by Perry and Beebe. This book was written in 1900 for young people. It's a great account of the lives of Daniel Boone, David Crockett, George Rogers Clark, and Kit Carson. Packed full of adventure, this is sure to be a favorite.

Uncle Rick Reads Heroes of Our Revolution by T. W. Hall. This book was written in 1900 and tells the true stories of so many of the heroes who fought in the War of Independence. Told in a captivating way that your kids will want to hear again and again.

Uncle Rick Reads Israel Putnam. No part of America's history is more exciting than the turbulent years of the Revolutionary War. And no man of the time saw more of danger and adventure than a Connecticut farmer who joined the patriot army and rose to fame as General Israel Putnam.

Uncle Rick Reads Jefferson's Masterpiece by Dennis Parker. *Jefferson's Masterpiece* is the narrative account of why and how the Declaration of Independence was written and approved. It takes young readers on a historical journey from June 11 to August 2, 1776. They follow Thomas Jefferson as he writes the Declaration of Independence and carries out his daily activities. For grades 4–8, but loved by younger children as well. (UncleRickAudios.com)

Uncle Rick Reads Marion's Men — The Swamp Fox! Was there ever a more exciting life than that of General Francis Marion, the wily swamp fighter of the Carolina colonies? With only a handful of men, Marion lurked in the shady depths of the southern marshes, emerging to strike like lightning at the forces of British General Cornwallis and then vanishing back into the dark forest. Always outnumbered, fighting with inferior weapons, starving and ragged, Marion's men nevertheless kept their extraordinary courage against all odds. Meeting overwhelming numbers of the enemy with bravery and cunning, these early American heroes were a constant thorn in the side of the mighty British army in the southern colonies. Their little force held Cornwallis in check, keeping him from joining the British forces fighting in the north against Washington. Seldom in history has such a small force of patriots done so much to win freedom for so many!

Uncle Rick Reads Old Put the Patriot. Join Uncle Rick as he follows Old Put through the many exciting adventures of his life and learn of the part he played in winning our freedom.

Uncle Rick Reads Petticoat Warriors. One of the lesser-known facts of our nation's history is the important role played by American women in our War for Independence from England. Now you can meet these great women and many others who endured great danger and sacrifice to bring freedom to America!

Uncle Rick Reads Revolutionary Heroes. A new nation is born! Thirteen feeble English colonies, disowned by their king and parliament, denied the rights and protections due them as Englishmen, take up arms against the mightiest nation on earth to fight for their freedom. They have no army, no navy, no treasury, no allies. But what they do have is a generation of men and women of superior wisdom and character, made strong by a deep faith in their God and the demands of living in a raw new land. Listen and be inspired as Uncle Rick reads the true story of some of the heroes who gave us America!

Uncle Rick Reads the Story of Great Americans for Young Americans. All children need heroes who will inspire them to dream big dreams and do great things. *True Stories of Great Americans for Young Americans* is a collection of exciting true accounts of the lives of great American men and women who made their mark on history and demonstrated worthy ideals for future generations to aspire to. Uncle Rick's friendly, informal style brings to colorful life some of America's brightest luminaries to entertain and inspire boys and girls everywhere!

Uncle Rick Reads the True Story of Ben Franklin. Perhaps no other American of his time was so well-known and accomplished so much in the interest of American independence as Benjamin Franklin. A signer of the Declaration of Independence and the Constitution, Franklin was also America's envoy to France and England, America's first Postmaster General, President of the Colony of PA, and even for a while a general in the PA militia. The epitome of the self-made American, Franklin acquired most of his superb and practical education by his own study.

Uncle Rick Reads The True Story of George Washington. He was called the Father of his Country: George Washington — soldier, surveyor, farmer, statesman — the epitome of the American hero. Now this American giant comes alive once again in this classic audio reproduction of the 1895 biography by famed historical writer Elbridge S. Brooks.

Uncle Rick Reads the True Story of Lafayette. He was a boy general. The young Marquis de Lafayette set sail for America in a ship purchased with his own money to cast his lot with George Washington's embattled citizen soldiers. Committing both his life and his fortune, Lafayette soon earned the great general's deep respect as well as his warm and lasting friendship. Always at the hottest point in the battle, yet never striving for his own glory, the youthful soldier proved both his courage and loyalty to the cause of freedom. When that freedom was won for his American comrades, he returned to his native France to spend the rest of his adventurous life fighting for the same "rights of the people" in his home country. Here is Lafayette — hero to the new American nation and a worthy model for young people of every generation.

Uncle Rick Reads Under Greene's Banner by T. C. Harbaugh. The struggle between the Tories and the Patriots in Piedmont Carolina during the Revolution forms the background for this spy story. The novel contains enough action scenes to hold a young reader's attention. The Battle of Guilford Courthouse is vividly depicted. Learn of Greene's role in the struggle for freedom. (Boys of Liberty Series)

Uncle Rick Reads Washington's Young Spy. Exciting! That's the word for the life of a spy. If caught, he will be hanged as a criminal. If he's successful, he will be a hero and his work may win the war for his country. Follow the breathtaking adventures of young Frank Lowry as he accepts the challenge of the great Washington and lays his life on the line for his beloved America. Share the thrills and the danger of the most challenging warfare of all — spying on the enemy in his own territory!

Uncle Rick Tells Stories of the Signers of the Declaration of Independence. These stories were originally published in 1908 for use in the public school as fifth/sixth-grade reading material. They are excellent patriotic stories of events that occurred during the War of Independence, such as the Boston Tea Party, and events that led to the war and people involved in it. They are fascinating for kids ages 5 to 13.

Uncle Rick Tells Stories of the War for Independence. These stories were originally published in 1908 for use in the public school as fifth/sixth-grade reading material. They are excellent patriotic stories of events that occurred during the War of Independence, such as the Boston Tea Party, and events that led to the war and the people involved in it. They are fascinating for kids ages 5 to 13.

BOOKS

Ben Franklin of Old Philadelphia by Margaret Cousins. Benjamin Franklin was one of the busiest men in the American colonies. He was a printer, postmaster, inventor, writer, and diplomat. When the Revolutionary War began, Ben supported America in the Continental Congress. Like the clever adages from his *Poor Richard's Almanac*, Ben Franklin still sets an example for Americans today. (Landmark Book, Grades 3 to 6)

The Boston Tea Party by Russell Freedman. More than any other event, the Boston Tea Party of 1773 has come to stand for the determination of American colonists to control their own destinies. From the arrival of the ships full of controversial taxed tea in Boston Harbor, through the meetings at the Old South Church, to the actual dumping of 226 chests of fine tea into the harbor on December 16, Freedman captures this exciting story. Grades 3 to 5.

The Bulletproof George Washington by David Barton. Colonial George Washington's perilous experiences in the French and Indian War are chronicled in this riveting account of God's providence and protection. The only officer on horseback to avoid being shot down, young Washington openly attributed his miraculous escape from harm to the intervention of a sovereign God. A story once found in student textbooks, this awe-inspiring adventure is recaptured in a modern edition complete with maps and illustrations. (Wallbuilders Press, 62 pages, paperback)

Caeser Rodney's Ride: The Story of an American Patriot by Jan Cheripko. Jan Cheripko presents the burning issues of that time, the men who fought for them, and the story of the great patriot whose breakneck ride for freedom served to ensure the birth of the United States. Grades 3 to 6.

Daniel Boone — American Adventure Series by Edna McGuire. The story of the growth of America is told in the deeds of men and women moving westward in search of new land, new homes, and greater opportunities. The sturdy pioneers settled frontiers and bravely defended them. They endured dangers and hardships to make these regions part of the United States. Daniel Boone was one of these freedom-loving, home-seeking pioneers. Again and again he pushed out to a new frontier. He fought boldly in defense of his home. He faced with high courage the hardships of the frontier. This story is written so that girls and boys may know Daniel Boone and understand the deeds of thousands of other pioneers like him. Their courage and daring made America a land of freedom and opportunity. Great for grades 4 to 6.

Daniel Boone — Taming the Wilds. An exciting biography of the frontier hero who first explored Kentucky and later opened passages to the West. For grades 2 to 5. (A Discovery Series reader)

For You They Signed: The Spiritual Heritage of Those Who Shaped our Nation by Marilyn Boyer. They pledged their lives, their fortunes, and their sacred honor so we could be free! More than simply facts and figures, *For You They Signed* provides an abundance of resources within one volume, including: a full year of life-changing, challenging family or group devotional character studies, over 90 illustrations, biographical summaries, insightful quotes, and character quality definitions. Great to read as a family. (Master Books)

The Founders: The 39 Stories Behind the U.S. Constitution by Dennis Fradin. Thirty-nine men ultimately signed this important, influential framework that saved our country and gave us our amazingly strong and balanced federal government. Dennis Brindell Fradin and Michael McCurdy combine their talents to bring all of the Founders' stories to light in this fascinating companion volume to their bestselling book *The Signers*. (Walker and Co)

Jefferson's Masterpiece is the narrative account of why and how the Declaration of Independence was written and approved. It takes young readers on a historical journey from June 11 to August 2, 1776. They follow Thomas Jefferson as he writes the Declaration of Independence and carries out his daily activities. For grades 4 to 8, but loved by younger children as well. Biographical summaries, insightful quotes, and character quality definitions. Great to read as a family.

John Paul Jones — American Adventure Series by Vinson Brown. You have read of the brave deeds of American pioneers in the forests, on the mountains, and across the plains. But others found adventure on the seas. Of these, John Paul Jones was the most famous. John Paul was a Scotch gardener's son, but his early love for the sea caused him to become a sailor. Later, he joined the Americans in their fight for justice and freedom. His skill and daring at sea helped win American independence in the Revolutionary War. John Paul Jones was at his best when he faced danger. His refusal to accept defeat became the spirit of the navy. He earned the proud title, "Father of the American Navy." Great series written for grades 4 to 6. (Wheeler Publishing Co.)

John Paul Jones — Sailor Hero by Stewart Graff. John Paul Jones was small and swift, even as the ships he commanded so successfully during the American Revolution. His daring raids, first on enemy vessels and then on the English coast itself, helped change the course of the Revolution and gave the struggling colonies prestige and glory. John Paul, the boy, growing up in a simple harbor town in Scotland, longed to go to sea. He was ambitious and dreamed of being a captain. He never dreamed his life would be as adventurous as it was, that he would choose a new country for his own, and give the American Navy "its earliest traditions of heroism and victory." From cabin boy voyages to the Caribbean, to the great battle between the *Bonhomme Richard* and the *Serapis*, this is an outstanding first book written with impact and vigor. (Discovery Series)

Let It Begin Here — Lexington and Concord by Dennis Fradin A crisply written, vivid, you-are-there account of Paul Revere's actions on the night of April 18, 1775. Great for grades 3 to 6. (CharacterConcepts.com)

A More Perfect Union: The Story of Our Constitution by Betsy Maestro. With accurate historical information, this easy-to-understand book tells why and how the Constitution of the United States was created. Includes a map and back matter with a table of dates and a summary of the Articles of the Constitution.

Portraits of Integrity by Marilyn Boyer and Grace Tumas. Tells the sacrificial story of General Caesar Rodney and his ride for independence! (The Learning Parent)

Profiles of Valor — Character Studies from the War of Independence by Marilyn Boyer and Grace Tumas. Stories include John Witherspoon and his persuasive speech for independence, Sam Adams and his role in obtaining liberty, as well as 38 other exciting stories of the War of Independence. (The Learning Parent)

Redcoats and Petticoats by Katherine Kirkpatrick. The story of Nancy Strong and her role with petticoats in the Culper Spy ring. (Holiday House)

The Signers: The 56 Stories Behind the Declaration of Independence. Who were these men who are the first heroes of our nation? Award-winning team of author Dennis Brindell Fradin and illustrator Michael McCurdy bring their considerable talents together to illuminate the lives of these valiant men, ranging from the poorest farmers to the wealthiest merchants, whose dauntless courage inspired thousands of colonists to risk all for freedom. Grades 4–6

We the People: The Story of Our Constitution by Lynne Cheney. Beautifully illustrated book that tells how our Constitution came to be. Grades 3–5 (CharacterConcepts.com)

● *What Would the Founding Fathers Think?* by David Bowman. Join Washington, Franklin, and Madison as they discuss our country's crisis as compared with their original intentions for America. With humor and a variety of visuals, David Bowman skillfully teaches the wisdom of returning to our nation's founding principles in a way that makes it easy to "get it." (Plain Sight Publishing)

E-BOOKS

Ben Franklin — Man of Ideas. Your children will be inspired when they read of all Ben Franklin accomplished in his lifetime and how what he did so greatly impacts us today. (A Discover Reader)

Lafayette — French American Hero. Everyone in our country used to know who Layfayette was. As a young freedom-loving Frenchman, he gave of his time and sacrificed by volunteering with our colonial forces to win against the might of the British Empire. He was appreciated and loved by all Americans for a very long time. You'll be amazed at his inspiring story. Great readers for grades 2 to 6. (Discovery Reader Series)

Daily Lesson Plans

WE'VE DONE THE WORK FOR YOU!

PERFORATED & 3-HOLE PUNCHED
FLEXIBLE 180-DAY SCHEDULE
DAILY LIST OF ACTIVITIES
RECORD KEEPING

"THE TEACHER GUIDE MAKES THINGS
SO MUCH EASIER AND TAKES THE
GUESS WORK OUT OF IT FOR ME."

HOMESCHOOL

Master Books® Homeschool Curriculum

Faith-Building Books & Resources
Parent-Friendly Lesson Plans
Biblically-Based Worldview
Affordably Priced

Master Books® is the leading publisher of books and resources
based upon a Biblical worldview that points to God as our Creator.
Now the books you love, from the authors you trust like Ken Ham, Michael Farris,
Tommy Mitchell, and many more are available as a homeschool curriculum.

MASTERBOOKS.COM
Where Faith Grows!